I'm a Woman
Created in the Image of God

By

Joyce Cope Wyatt

I'm a Woman Created in the Image of God
Published originally in Spanish. Copyright © 1988. Used with permission by
Editorial Mundo Hispano, 7000 Alabama St., El Paso, Texas 79904 USA.

English version Copyright © 2010 by BWA Women's Department.

ISBN 978-0-9763445-2-0

Published by BWA Women's Department

Additional copies of this book may be purchased from:
BWA Women's Department
405 North Washington Street
Falls Church, VA 22046
Tel: +1-703-790-8980 Ext. 4
Fax: +1-703-903-9544
www.bwanet.org

Front cover designed by Andrew Chee. Photo by Marcos Santos.

Printed in the USA by Bethany Press International.

Dedication

To my mother, my sister

and my two daughters,

each of whom has helped me in

my formation as a woman;

and

to the women

of the Spanish-speaking world,

my co-laborers in ministry for more than thirty years.

DEDICATION OF THE ENGLISH VERSION

To the women of the Baptist World Alliance

Women's Department,

Inspiration, blessing and challenge

in my life

and that of countless others all over the world.

Contents

Preface to the English Edition

Twenty years following the publication of this book in Spanish, the Women's Department of the Baptist World Alliance voted to authorize its publication in English to be used as a resource for women all over the world. The Spanish version has been reprinted on six occasions, the last edition in 1999. It is now available in a CD in Spanish, *La Biblioteca de la Mujer* (A Library for Women). In these many editions and in its present form, *Soy Mujer! Soy Especial!* continues to give a sound understanding of the role of Christian women in the different areas of their lives. Its basic premise that women are created in God's image and likeness is valid for all time, and for which we continue to give thanks to Him.

In July of 2008 I was invited to join a team from the Baptist World Alliance Women's Department to visit Sofía, Bulgaria, for a meeting with Baptist women from the whole country. It was a blessed experience as we met with about a hundred women, many of whom had suffered for their faith, and others who had come to know Christ through the faithfulness of these older women.

BWA Women's Department Director Patsy Davis, who had been a missionary in Venezuela and had used the teachings of this book there, continued to do so in her international role as she traveled to different countries on every continent and shared its liberating Christian message for women. On the occasion of our being in Bulgaria she asked me to bring two messages on the Christian woman from the teachings of the book. As a result the decision was made to publish the book in English so that it might be available to a larger number of women throughout the Baptist world.

My special thanks to the Executive Committee of the Women's Department of the Baptist World Alliance for their expression of confidence in me and in the message of this book. As I have translated it into English I am convinced that its message is as valid today as it was when first presented in Panama. While the book in essence is the same as published in 1988, I have taken the liberty to include limited additional information which I feel will enhance its message and its ministry today and in the future.

I pray that as this new edition reaches women on every continent that it will be seen as Good News. May God use it to light your pathway to a deeper understanding of your place in His kingdom as a woman created in His image, and may you have the courage to follow your Lord in every area of your life.

I am grateful to our daughter, Debbi Wyatt Christinck, who is a reporter and a special woman in her own right, for her help in reading and editing the English copy.

With affection and gratitude,

Joyce Cope Wyatt

Preface

This book has been "in process" for many years, perhaps all my life. I have always liked to think, to question, to learn, and to find more meaning for my life. I love creative ideas, stimulating books, interesting conversations, and experiences that open more possibilities for reflection, action and growth.

From my early years as a missionary I have had the opportunity to teach, write articles, present conferences, give studies and facilitate learning on a great diversity of themes, frequently in some specific facet of women's life and experience. I have continued to read, study, and investigate women's life experience. As a result I have become more aware of the reality of women in the Spanish-speaking world, as well as that of women in other parts of the world. I have sought answers to my questions in accord with the teachings of Christ, and therefore my life as a woman has been enriched. Without a doubt today my ideas about women are healthier, more freeing, more Christian that in previous stages of my life, for which I am very grateful.

In 1984 I was invited to give eight conferences for the week-long annual meeting of Women's Missionary Union of Panama on the subject, "I'm a Woman! I'm Special!" These conferences were greatly blessed by our Lord and were received by these dear sisters in Christ with enthusiasm and gratitude. Their appreciation for the focus on the Christian woman given in these conferences and their desire to have them in printed form stimulated me to want to use them with other groups, and to make them available to the largest audience possible. Now, thanks to the Spanish Baptist Publishing House, and especially to my friend and editor Mary Jo Stewart, this dream has become a reality. I am aware that this book would never have been published had it not been for the affirmation and support of Christian women in Panama, Colombia, Venezuela and Ecuador where I have been able to share this basic focus on the Christian woman personally. I extend to each of them my deepest gratitude.

I appreciate the understanding of my husband, Roy, of my commitment to the preparation of this book and for His help in coming to a deeper understanding of many of the biblical passages that are basic to the ideas that are developed here.

I thank God for His constant guidance and for His great kindness and mercy shown me in the preparation and development of this book. I pray that it will be an instrument of blessing in the life of every woman who reads it.

Joyce Cope de Wyatt

1. Made in the Image of God

> *"And God said, 'Let Us make humankind in Our*
> *image, according to Our likeness'... So God*
> *created humankind in His image, and in the*
> *image of God He created them, male and female He*
> *created them. God blessed them." Genesis 1:26-28a*

Have you ever thought about who you are? Who you <u>really</u> are? As Christian women this is one of the most important things we will ever do. This book will help you as you start on this life-changing and life-affirming journey. To start, we can say, "I'm a woman! I'm a Christian woman! I'm special." As a result of these affirmations you have a perspective about your life and of whom you are that many other women don't have. Not only are you made in the image of God, but, also, since you are a Christian, you can grow in Christ and become more of what He would have you be. You can grow more and more in the image of God!

When you became a Christian you became a new creature as John tells us in his Gospel:

> "But to all who received Him, who believed in His name,
> He gave power to become children of God." John 1:12

Thus you are special; you are a child, a daughter, of God. You are special in your relationship with God, your Heavenly Father.

The plan of God in creation - Genesis 1

It is impossible to believe that God did not have a grand plan for the creation of the world in which we live. Just reading the first chapter of Genesis fills us with awe at the marvel of God's creation. The action of God in the creation of stage after stage, each of which is followed by His declaration, "It is good," helps us see the reality of God's plan and the special purpose He has in creation. In the moment of the creation of man and woman, God said,

> "Let Us make humankind in Our image, according to
> Our likeness...." So God created humankind in His
> image, and in the image of God He created them, male
> and female He created them. God blessed them."
> Genesis 1:26-28a

What does it mean to be made in God's image? Both man and woman received certain qualities that make them distinct from the animals that God had created. While these qualities include the capacity to control or domesticate animals, personally I believe that to be created in God's image refers to our spiritual qualities, because God is Spirit. As persons made in His image, we can have communion with God; we can know Him, do His will, be responsible to Him, and make the decision to obey Him or to disobey Him. And if this is not enough, we are affirmed as the crown of His creation and thus the highest representative of God, our Creator. We are truly blessed for we are His creation, made in His image.

To be created in God's image refers to our spiritual qualities

From the very beginning the plan of God was that man and woman should be His collaborators in the world, His representatives in the care and conscientious use of all that He had created. The Bible says that God blessed man and woman whom He had created and gave them the blessing and the responsibility of procreation, of having dominion over the earth, to rule over the animals, birds and fish. As a loving father, almost with a maternal care, He explained to them what they should eat! After viewing all that He had made, God recognized "that it was very good" (Genesis 1:31.) It is very interesting that after this creative activity, God rested, another way in which we need to emulate His priorities.

Man and woman, both created in His image
- Genesis 2

The first two chapters of Genesis give two distinct interpretations or accounts of creation. Some have considered the second chapter as evidence that woman is inferior to man. However, when the difference between the two accounts is fully appreciated, this confusion should no longer exist.

Two times in Genesis, in 1:27 and in 5:1-2, the creation of both man and woman is confirmed as made in the image of God. The magnificent account in Genesis 1 gives purpose and significance to life, both for women as well as for men. It emphasizes the importance of being in relationship with God, and with other human beings.

But, what about Genesis 2? Here we see God concerned for the man (*adam*) whom He has created out of the soil of the earth (*adamah*). God recognizes the loneliness of the man He has formed, a loneliness that cannot be satisfied by the animals he has named. He must be provided with "a helper like himself", one who corresponds to him, one who is appropriate for him, "a helper suitable for him." (Genesis 2:18).

The most important teaching of this passage has to do with the relationship between man and woman. However, if in reading this passage you conclude, "Frankly, it seems to me that the creation of woman is like an afterthought on God's part, and was not in His original plan," then you will have serious problems about the role of women in your life. But, thank God, this is not the correct interpretation. The role of women should be seen as God Himself conceived it: a companion for the companion, the couple related in mutual love and consideration. The earth-creature needed to have a companion who was neither superior to him nor inferior to him, but one who would eliminate his solitary condition and his isolation, and with whom each would be able to encounter his or her true identity.

In Genesis 2:23 the Hebrew is very graphic in the words in which Adam expresses his joy, "Oh, yes. This is the helper I really need."

> "This at last is bone of my bones and flesh of my flesh.
> This one shall be called Woman, for out of Man this one was taken."

Adam is ecstatic; he has a companion! His joyous affirmation is evidence that he sees that this woman is exactly what he needs. As a result Adam gives names both for himself and for the woman. These are names that show their relationship, man and wo-man (*ish and ishah*), two creatures now ready for relationship. The attraction of each for the other is so strong that "man will leave his mother and father and unite with his wife, and the two will be one" (Genesis 2:24.) There will not only be sexual union, but social and intellectual companionship. Now man will not be alone for he has his companion, exactly what he was lacking. In this act we see the harmony created by God for this couple: a sense of unity, of totality, of completeness in community and relationship.

It is interesting that the idea of "rule over" the earth is not found in Genesis 2, but the words which are used are "labor" and "guard" God's creation. Another evidence, perhaps, of the emphasis here of relationship and harmony in the community: a more complete and holistic relationship with God, with nature, with animal life, and with one's companion.

The word "help meet" used in the King James Version, and much later "helpmate" in the New Jerusalem Bible, has been used to give a false interpretation to this concept. The word does not signify a servant, an apprentice, or a slave. Never forget the reason God created woman as recorded in Genesis 2. The reason was so that "man would not be alone." He needed someone who would be able to relate to him, one who could fill this need. Old Testament scholars teach that the Hebrew word "alone" or to "be alone" means to be "lost, helpless, abandoned, without help." Man and woman, created in God's image, have been created to live in community, in relationship one to the other. Rather than helpless one finds a helper, rather than loneliness one finds companionship.

Another concept that can help us appreciate the true meaning of "help meet" is to consider the role of God as help to those in need. In the Old Testament God is spoken of as "a present help in time of trouble" (Psalm 46:1) and "Blessed is the man whose help is the God of Jacob" (Psalm 146:5). The presence of Christ and of the Holy Spirit, our constant help, gives even more emphasis to the importance of this word and concept. It is interesting that in the Old Testament the word "help" (*ezer*) is used twenty-one times, sixteen of which are used in reference to God, two times in reference to the woman, as seen here, and three times in reference to man.

When God created man and woman He created two helpers who were to be companions to each other. This teaches us the importance of living in community. As God is a companion to humanity, so man and woman are companions to one another. The rights of human beings created to represent God in the world carry with them the responsibility to relate one to another and to God. When we speak of the "rights" of men and the "responsibilities" of women, we "miss the mark" of our common shared and God-given humanity. Each has rights, and each has responsibilities in relationship.

In Christ we can affirm that the God who created us to both need and give help, is the same God who is our helper. To be a "help meet," or a "helper suitable" for another, is to share the life of another person, being for him or her the help that is needed - a concept that has come from the very heart of God!

A little lower than God - Psalm 8

Psalm 8 is a psalm praising God as Creator, His majesty and His glory. It also proclaims the special place given human beings in creation, as well as the privileges and responsibilities given to them by their Creator. The glory of humanity is that we, women and men, have been made in the image of God. Thus we must honor Him and bring glory to His Name by the way we live, so that others may see His presence in us. Since we are made to be in relationship with God, this relationship should be seen in our daily lives, reflecting the depth of our spirituality and our commitment to doing His will.

We glorify God by living as He would have us live, remembering that we are created in His image and as a result have a vision of what He expects of us as citizens of His kingdom. Old Testament theologian Jürgen Moltman[1] says that in order to bring change to the world we must develop what he calls a "utopian consciousness," one that seeks a more humane reality for all people, where forms of social oppression and dehumanization are criticized and actions are taken to produce a more just and liberating society. When we believe in God and His plan for the world, we can join Him in this task and share the hope for a better, more just world.

The psalmist is amazed that God, this great God who has created such a majestic universe, should give humanity such importance, creating men and women in His image and giving each of them so many responsibilities, crowning each with glory and honor. When you recognize God's role in your life in these ways, and you worship and serve Him to reflect His glory, your life becomes a part of this psalm of praise. However, created "a little lower than God" does not give you the right to "lord it over" creation or over another person, but rather, knowing you are wonderfully made, to live responsibly as God's creation.

The perversion of the image of God - Genesis 3

Genesis 3 presents a sad picture of "Paradise Lost." In reality what was lost was much more than Paradise. Hope was lost; a part of God's grand plan for the world and for humankind was lost. Theologian Phyllis Tribble describes it in these words:

> "Where once there was mutuality, now there is a hierarchy
> of division. The man dominates the woman to pervert sexuality.

Hence, the woman is corrupted in becoming a slave, and man is corrupted, becoming a master."[2]

In the fall of humanity, both man and woman had lost their special relationship with God, who had created them. Instead of continuing to be His special representatives on the earth, they wanted to become "like God" and they leave Paradise devastated and deviated from the original plan of God. Instead of working and caring for the garden where everything was beautiful and easy to care for, they would have to work hard to produce sustenance from the earth in order that they might survive. It is important to read these passages carefully in order to note that God does not curse the man or the woman, but the serpent, the deceiver, and the earth which no longer will be a lush and productive paradise, but one that produces thorns and weeds. Only by arduous sweat-producing labor will the land produce food.

Today we continue in the steps of our first parents. We, too, try to take God out of the picture, to take away His leadership and replace it with our own. In doing so, we are the ones who become dislocated for we lose our place in the plan of God. When we break the ties of relationship that we have with our Creator, our Heavenly Father, we also lose our sense of solidarity with others. We are alone. We are lost!

God will complete the good work begun in you
- Philippians 1:6b

In the New Testament there are many passages that speak of the image of God in the person of Christ. The writer of Hebrews describes Him as, "the reflection of God's glory and the exact imprint of God's very being" (Hebrews 1:3a.) Paul says, "He is the image of the invisible God," (Colossians 1:15a) and "Christ, who is the image of God" (2 Corinthians 4:4c.) In these passages we see another dimension of our relationship with God in whose image we are created. In Christ we can expand our understanding of our self-image for we can identify with Him, the perfect image of God.

To be a Christian means to change from how we were before to what we are now and what we will become in the future. "...you have stripped off the old self with its practices, and have clothed yourselves with the new self, which is being renewed in knowledge according to the image of its Creator" (Colossians 3:9b, 10).

This new reality is the result of our constant communion with Christ, our Savior. "And all of us, with unveiled faces, seeing the glory of the Lord as though reflected in a mirror, are being transformed into the same image from one degree of glory to another; for this comes from the Lord, the Spirit" (2 Corinthians 3:18).

The process of growing in the image of Christ depends on our intimate relationship with Him. But we are not alone, for He works with and for us in this daily experience. Paul assures us "that the One who began a good work among you will bring it to completion by the day of Jesus Christ" (Philippians 1:6). We can rejoice because we have been created in the image of God and now, in Christ, we have the possibility of living this image in our daily life. As we grow in Him daily we press toward becoming the woman God wants us to be.

John gives us a vision of this process that can serve as a challenge for our journey. It helps us see that we have come from a previous stage so that we can rejoice in what we are now, and anticipate what we will become in the future, recognizing that all of this is a growth process in which we have been led and helped by our loving Heavenly Father.

> "See what love the Father has given us, that we should
> be called children of God; and that is what we are. The reason
> the world does not know us is that it did not know Him.
> Beloved, we are God's children now; what we will be has
> not yet been revealed. What we do know is this: when He is
> revealed, we will be like Him, for we shall see Him as He is.
> And all who have this hope in Him purify themselves, just as He
> is pure" (1 John 3:1-3).

I'm a woman! I'm special! I am made in the image of God to live and grow in relationship with Him. I'm a woman, created in the image of God and growing in that image through my relationship with Christ.

Activities for reflection and learning

1. Write a psalm of praise to God for having been created in His image and likeness.

   Mention experiences and attitudes that give evidence that you are created in His image and how you are growing into that image. Perhaps you could read some psalms before writing your own, including Psalms 8 and 139.

2. Study 1 John 3:1-3 using the inductive method. What does this passage mean to you as a child of God who is developing in His image? Write down your feelings as a result of this reflection as well as the challenges you face as a child of God.

Questions to answer alone or in a group:

• What does it mean to you to be created in God's image? Note several characteristics that you believe should be seen in a woman who affirms that she is made in God's image. Are these seen in your life? How can you increasingly show that you are made in God's image and likeness?

• Describe some ways in which women are characterized on television or in other forms of media. How do these characterizations influence you as a woman? Do they influence women at one particular age or stage more than another? Who is most vulnerable to them? What can you do to bring a more balanced depiction of women in the media?

• What can you do to become more authentic to who you are in God's sight? List specific steps that you can take.

2. In Search of My Identity

"The Lord called me before I was born,
while I was in my mother's womb He named me....
And He said to me, 'You are my servant, Israel,
in whom I will be glorified.'"
Isaiah 49:1b, 3

As Christian women we find our identity in God and in His plan for us as His beloved daughters. From the beginning, in His plan in creation, God established the value of every person who lived then or would live in the future, because each of us is made in His image. Someone has said that one of the reasons why we should return to study the first chapters of the Bible is to recognize where we once were, and how to again recapture our place in the plan of God for His creation.

Even though God places such a high value on every human being, nevertheless there are Christian women who have such a poor self-concept that they can't even conceive of the idea that God might talk to them, call them and use them in His work. This is not the idea of "not being worthy", but rather the idea of being a person who sees herself as totally without value and significance. Without an adequate sense of identity we will not allow ourselves to hear the voice of God and His call to become all He intends us to be as His special creation.

As Christian women our identity has its foundation in God and in His concept of who we are. When we have a self-concept with such a firm foundation as this we will be able to develop into persons who are truly human, truly God's child as well as His servant.

Who am I?

One of most important and most difficult questions a Christian woman needs to answer is, "Who am I?" As Christians we should begin our answer affirming, "I'm a woman made in God's image, saved by His Son Jesus Christ, guided and comforted by the Holy Spirit, and His co-laborer in His Kingdom." However, even though we believe this intellectually, or we can affirm it when other Christians talk to us about it, in many cases we do not show it in our daily living, nor do we consider it to be who we truly are.

One way to express our theological belief that we are created in God's image is the self-esteem we show when we accept our uniqueness as a person. I am an individual; I am unique. There is not another person in the world exactly like me. How, then, can I live in such a way that I am truly becoming myself – the woman God desires me to become? To begin with, I must accept my responsibility to form my own individuality. This is the child's first challenge.

In the first weeks of life our individuality is not evidenced. The infant still considers herself as part of her mother's body and her survival depends on this very intimate relationship. It is later, during the first months of life, when the infant begins to sense her separateness from the mother and simultaneously begins to develop confidence in her and in others. The lack of positive experiences of trust with the mother and other significant persons during this early period of life will produce a child who is unable to trust others, and who will often carry this problem of mistrust into adulthood. It has been said that the first right of an infant is to have a trustworthy mother.

Famed psychologist Gordon Allport[3] says that there are three aspects of our self-awareness that are developed gradually during the first three years of life and that remain with a person during the rest of her life:

1. The sense of bodily self.
2. The sense of a continuing self-identity.
3. The sense of self-esteem or pride.

Our sense of bodily self begins when the baby realizes that she has hands, feet, a face, and other parts of the body, discovering in this way that she is more than just an extension of the mother. From this time on the child develops a sense of pride or of shame about her body, many times in an exaggerated way. This early-formed concept is carried with them, often to their detriment, through the rest of their lives. Many women base their self-concept to a large degree on their body concept, on how they see their body, much of it internalized in her early years.

As children grow and begin to realize that they are persons distinct from others, they begin to develop their own individual identity. In this period it seems that "mine" and "me" are favorite words. It's not that they necessarily want to be stubborn, difficult and non-cooperative, but they are trying to find out just what the parameters of their newly found identity are.

One very important element of the development of self-identity is the name that is given to the child and how the child is addressed. In the Bible the name of the person is very important. It signifies the essence of who the person is. For this reason parents thought long and hard before naming a child, because the name would not only influence her self- concept, but also would place and help form her in the paths of the Lord. Our name gives significance to our life and through its repeated use personality is developed. We come to realize that we are individuals, separate from others through the use of our name.

Many people have a very inferior concept of their self-identity because their parents, or others, have spoken to them disparagingly, calling them "stupid," "ugly," "fool," or other such derogatory statements. As a result they have internalized these words as their identity. They are convinced that they are worthless and "can't do anything right" since they have been "named" and spoken to in these ways during their childhood and beyond.

Our name gives significance to our life

As children begin to feel their own individuality and begin to esteem themselves and their abilities more, they want to do more things by themselves, to develop their own capacities. It is a difficult period for parents because it is challenging to teach or lead them when they are developing this independence. A wise rabbi said that the correct interpretation of Proverbs 22:6 is, "Train a child in the way <u>he</u> should go, and when he is old he will not turn from it" (NIV). That is, every person has a way in which they should develop their own individuality. Each has different interests, different abilities, and different ways of learning, of working, and of being. Parents who recognize this truth and <u>know</u> their children in this way will be able to give them better instruction and formation, and the child will be blessed.

The development of our identity is a life-long task, but it is built on these early childhood experiences. However, this is not the whole story. From a theological perspective we are called by God to join Him in a covenant of service and companionship. As we enter into this covenant we continue to develop our individuality. The Christian should not say, "I'm the way I am because my parents were this way," or "because they treated me in this way."

Each person is responsible for who she is, for the way in which she has used the experiences of her childhood and youth in the development of her identity and her individuality, and how she will continue to do so the rest of her life. But, take heart! God works with us in this task. One very special name for Jesus is Emmanuel, "God with us"- God with us in the search for, the finding and the development of our own identity.

How to maintain my identity as I relate to others

When we do not know who we are, we are vulnerable, not only with others who may control or manipulate us, but also in the temptation to control or manipulate others. But when we are vulnerable and we know it, in that very moment God can help us by our openness to Him. As we more fully understand our own humanity, we come to recognize our need to maintain relationship with others. Who we are as human beings depends in part on the way in which we recognize and respect the rights of others around us and in the entire world.

Theologian Letty Russell in her book, *Becoming Human[4]*, says that there are three essential ingredients in order to maintain life on a human level, of "keeping life human." In times of such dehumanization as in today's world, these are of incalculable value for us as Christian women.

1. In order to keep human life human, first there is the need to be treated as a *subject* and not as an *object*. In today's world many women are treated as an object. They are a "non-person" in many families and societies influenced by this totally inhuman philosophy. These women are faceless, nameless, and valueless. God never treats a person as an object, but always as a subject, as a person of great value to Him and His plan for His creation. God loves each person, each individual, and He calls us by our name. (See Isaiah 43:1-3a.)

2. In order to keep human life human there must be the possibility of *participation in shaping our own future.* Since we express our humanity through the creation and meaning of our own life story we lose this essential element of being human when we live our lives as one with no hope. There are many women who never have an opportunity to express their own ideas about their future. Their families, their society, their work, and/or their church tell them who and what they are, and what they are to be. They have

no input. These women will always have a sense of emptiness and vacuum as they try to consider who they are.

However, it has been proven in the most difficult and inhuman situations that a person who has hope is able to confront life with courage, because they do have hope for the future. So, when we know that we can participate in the decisions about our own development and future, life takes on a different dimension. It is valuable, it has a new significance, it is more human.

3. The third essential ingredient for keeping human life human is to have a *community of support* where we can sense love and encouragement, where we are treated as a *subject* and never as an *object,* and where we are supported in our participation in the formation of our own future and the future of the group. Russell says that the church – as a community of believers and as the body of Christ – offers each person the support she needs in the search for her own humanity and development. In such a setting all are treated as persons of value, created in God's image, with hope for the future.

One of the most horrible experiences of life is to be alone, completely alone. The most effective punishment of prisoners in correctional institutions is that of solitary confinement. The prisoner who is isolated for periods of time can be controlled, for she becomes a *non-person,* and the traces of her identity are diminished. Eventually she is totally de-humanized. However, this problem is not found just with those who are incarcerated. There are many people in the world who experience extreme loneliness even though they are members of families and of churches, but their aloneness is etched deeply in their personalities and in their souls. They desperately need a sense of belonging, a sense of community of which they can be a part.

The church as a community of believers and as the body of Christ, must offer the believer this support of fellowship and friendship where each person can search for her own humanity and can work with others for the development of a more human and just treatment for all.

We maintain our identity as authentic human beings when we affirm our own humanity, when we reject the dehumanization so prevalent in our society and when we treat others in ways that affirm their humanity and dignity as a person created in God's image. In doing so, we, too, become more and more human, more the person God intends us to be.

In this day and time when many women, including Christian women, struggle with who they are and "try to find themselves," another author, Naomi Rosenblatt[5], a Jewish psychotherapist and Bible scholar, in her wonderful book on Genesis, *Wrestling with Angels,* says that we are never alone or anonymous when we know that we are created in God's image. Our identity is in Him, the identity He has given us in His great love and through His desire that we might have fellowship with Him and work with Him in bringing about a more truly human and just society. As long as we keep this core identity within us we can face whatever event may come our way without losing our sense of self and of our relatedness to God.

God, my helper in my search for my identity

I have no doubt that God's message to us is that we are special to Him. We are women created in His image and likeness, women who have been given His breath of life, and who have a special place in His plan for humanity. This is emphasized and re-emphasized in the New Testament. The heart of the New Testament is that God so loved each of us that He gave His only Son that we might believe on Him and thus receive eternal life. Jesus gave His life for us, and He promises us that He will be with us forever through the Holy Spirit which is His presence living in us. God wants all who follow in His footsteps to have the opportunity to grow and develop our potentiality. Each of us is a person of great value because:

> **We are made in God's image and likeness.**
> **We are saved by Christ's sacrifice on our behalf.**
> **We have the Holy Spirit, who makes His home in us.**

God has not forgotten His purpose for us; He is actively bringing it about. He is ready to affirm our identity and our relationship with Him. One of the passages that is foundational to our self-acceptance is found in Romans 8:15-17:

> "For you did not receive a spirit of slavery to fall back
> into fear, but you received a spirit of adoption.
> When we cry, 'Abba, Father!' it is that very Spirit
> bearing witness with our spirit that we are children
> of God, and if children, then heirs, heirs
> of God and joint-heirs with Christ - if, in fact, we
> suffer with Him so that we may also be glorified with Him."

In her book, *Gift from the Sea,* Anne Marrow Lindbergh[6] speaks of women's development throughout the different stages of their lives. She emphasizes that one of the greatest needs of women is to be whole, to be healthy, to be a complete person. The best way of developing this sense of wholeness is to spend time alone with God. This relationship permits her to renew herself as a person, to redevelop her individuality and to sense and affirm that she is a complete person. But many women's lives are fragmented; they are broken into pieces like a vase or jar. The Christian woman does not have to be destroyed in this way. She needs to be whole, not fragmented. To have a healthy and well-integrated personality, she needs to be clear about her identity. She needs to know who she really is.

The Bible is full of examples of God as our helper, the one who makes us whole. The Old Testament repeats many times how God enters in the daily lives of His followers to help them, to accompany them, to heal them, to give them hope. One such passage, and a very significant one, is found in Psalm 103:1-5:

> Bless the Lord, O my soul;
>   and all that is within me, bless His holy name.
> Bless the Lord, O my soul,
>   and do not forget all His benefits -
> who forgives all your iniquity,
>   who heals all your diseases,
> who redeems your life from the Pit
>   who crowns you with steadfast love and mercy,
>   who satisfies you with good as long as you live
>   so that your youth is renewed like the eagle's.

The psalmist captures in poetic form the reality of the activity of God as He works to bless us, making our life ever more human and significant.

You can find passage after passage in the four Gospels that show how important holistic health was to Christ as He met the needs of those who came to Him seeking the healing that only He could bring. One such passage is found in Luke 13:10-17. Eighteen years this woman was bent over and could not straighten up at all. Her situation was sad and critical; her life was "in pieces," fragmented, limited and painful. While the physical anguish was great, the spiritual and emotional anguish were even greater, for people believed that all suffering was the result of God's punishment for some sin or sins that the person had committed. As a result, the person who had an illness or disability was looked down on and ostracized from society.

This "in pieces," bent over woman could not do the things that a healthy woman could do. Certainly her situation must have been almost unbearable for it had been going on for eighteen long years. In all probability she was not treated as a person, but as a problem for her family, useless, and sinful. They believed that this was the way God punished sin.

But now, the miracle! In this environment where women were considered of little or no value, especially a physically handicapped woman, in this environment where men did not speak to women in public, where they would never touch a woman such as this because it would mean that they would become impure and would not be able to participate in religious activities, in this environment in which the observance of the Sabbath was more important than that of the needs of a person, in this negative environment Jesus responded with a miracle.

We, too, can be gifted with the five special blessings that Jesus gave this woman that Sabbath so long ago, blessing after blessing producing wholeness in this "in pieces," bent-over woman. When we consider how the synagogue was structured, we know that men and women were separated, the women at the back or side, behind a curtain or screen where they were neither seen nor heard. And yet, the **first blessing** is that Jesus "saw" her. He saw this poor woman, probably isolated and on the edge of the group. He had to have gone out of His way and made a special effort to do so. But that is how Jesus is: seeing the person in need and responding with love and care.

The **second blessing** is that He speaks to her. Men did not do that in those days. To speak to woman meant that you were lowering yourself to her status, someone without a brain, without knowledge, a "non-person." Yet Jesus **speaks** to her, calling her to come forward.

The **third blessing** is even more daring. He puts His hands on her; He touches her! In those days you did not touch a person who had an illness for fear of becoming unclean. Jesus knew the healing impact of human touch and what it must have meant to this woman who had probably not been touched by human hands for eighteen years.

With this touch and His words, the **fourth blessing** follows – He healed her! And "immediately she straightened up and praised God." She could stand up, she could look in the face of others, she could see the kindness of the One who had healed her. Of course, she praised God!

But not all were so pleased. The leader, the "ruler" of the synagogue, was indignant that Jesus had desecrated the Sabbath in this way and he rebuked

Him. Jesus responded by calling him a hypocrite and reminding the audience that even on the Sabbath they take care of their animals, "And ought not this woman, <u>a daughter of Abraham</u>, whom Satan bound for eighteen long years, be set free from this bondage on the Sabbath day?" And here we find the **fifth blessing:** Jesus makes her a part of the family! No longer is she isolated and marginalized by her illness. She is a daughter of Father Abraham! This is the only place in the New Testament that speaks of a woman as a "daughter of Abraham." What a boost to her self-esteem! She no longer was a non-person but a person tenderly cared for by the Master. This is precisely what Jesus does for women then and now. He makes us a part of the family of God!

There is no doubt that this woman was healed and made a whole person. She praised God for her new life. I believe Jesus is giving these five blessings to women who turn to Him in their need today, women who find Him as a result of some caring woman who shares this "good news" with them. Yes, Jesus loves you. He wants to heal you, to give your life meaning and purpose, for you are so special to Him.

We need to know who we really are

To this woman, "a non-person," Jesus gave not only life, but life abundant. But she is not the only one. What about Zacchaeus, or Matthew, or Mary Magdalene, or Peter, or the woman caught in adultery? All received a new identity given by the touch of Christ in their lives. Jesus said, "I came that they may have life, and have it abundantly" (John 10:10b). We can believe that He would tell us also, "I have come that you may find your true identity, and that you may have it to the full." Remember His words, "I will not leave you orphaned, I am coming to you" (John 14:18), "Abide in Me as I abide in you" (John 15:4a) and "Remember, I am with you always, to the end of the age" (Matthew 28:20b).

As Christian women we need to know who we really are. We need to work toward becoming more and more human in our relationship with others, and to recognize that God is our constant helper in our search for, and in our finding, our true identity. His challenge to us is that we might know Him more completely, more intimately, reading and following His Word, and talking and walking with Him daily so that we may become healthy and whole women, convinced of our humanity and our Christian identity.

Activities for reflection and learning

1. Many families, localities or institutions have shields that identify them as distinct from others. Make a copy of the following shield that will represent you and your identity as a person. Divide the shield into four sections to represent four aspects of your life. Then draw in each quadrant something that is representative of your life in that area. The following is one suggestion of aspects of your life that could be represented:

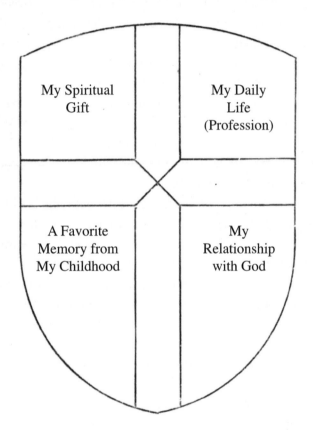

My Spiritual Gift

My Daily Life (Profession)

A Favorite Memory from My Childhood

My Relationship with God

(Other areas of your life can be combined for your shield.)

When you have completed the shield, think about why you chose each representation. Show your shield to a close friend to find out if she considers your shield a truthful presentation of who you are. Would she use different ways to describe who you are? Often we are able to find out more about ourselves through the eyes of others.

2. Make a list of personal attitudes that you consider important to be able to relate to others in a more human way. Then, using this list, grade yourself according to the way you show these attitudes as you relate to others.

3. Study John 4:1-42. Do you see the process of humanization developing in the Samaritan woman? List the steps you see as she slowly changes from a person who gives evidence of her alienation from the community to a woman who knows who she is and values her ability to share the gospel with her community. What can you learn from this process that can be applied to your personal life?

Questions to answer alone or in a group

• What does it mean to you to know who you are as a person?

• Do you believe that God has helped you in the process of bringing forth your identity as a person? Give specific examples of how you have experienced His action in your life.

• Do you feel that God wants to continue to help you to develop your true identity?

What does He want to do in your life? Are you willing to follow Him in these ways?

3. In My Spiritual Development

*"As you therefore have received Christ Jesus the Lord,
continue to live your lives in Him, rooted and built up in
Him and established in the faith, just as you were taught,
abounding in thanksgiving." Colossians 2:6-7*

When you read the Bible you find many passages that show how God rejects religious practices that have no meaning (Isaiah 1:11-18; Jeremiah 6:20; Amos 4:4-5; 5:21-24), hypocrisy in religion (Luke 11:42-44; Matthew 6:1-16), and harmful activities done in the name of religion (Luke 22:1-6; John18:19-24; Acts 26:9-11).

Contrary to all of these practices that are so hypocritical and harmful, Jesus brings a new message of hope and change, "Let anyone who is thirsty come to Me and let the one who believes in Me drink. As the Scripture has said, 'Out of the believer's heart shall flow rivers of living water'" (John 7:37b-38). The true experience of salvation is dynamic, life-giving, and lifelong. It opens the way for each person to grow and to develop their faith in authentic and profound ways.

The foundation: my relationship with Jesus

What does it mean to you to have faith? Is it to believe in something or someone? Is it a creed, or certain beliefs that are especially important for you? Faith includes these, but basically faith is the commitment of our lives, a commitment which gives them meaning and significance. For the believer, our commitment is with Christ, our Savior. Our faith finds meaning with Him and in Him. The community in which we develop our faith is an agent of blessing for us and for the body of Christ. It helps us affirm the principle values and beliefs of the Christian life and it strengthens the body as we all grow in faith and share our lives with one another. Our faith becomes the basic orientation for our life. For us as believers it is our faith in God that gives life and relationships their meaning and value.

The author of Hebrews gives the classic definition of faith: "Now faith is the assurance of things hoped for, the conviction of things not seen" (Hebrews 11:1). In order to have this Christian faith we must have made a commitment to Christ as our Savior, and in order to enter into this commitment we must accept His offer of salvation and make Him the Lord of our life. "For by grace you have been saved through faith, and this is not your own doing; it is the gift of God – not the result of works, so that no one may boast" (Ephesians 2:8-9).

Paul emphasizes three ideas in this passage: grace, the loving initiative of God to save; faith, the response to this initiative; and salvation, the great gift of God. The word salvation comes from the same root for the word that means health, well, complete or whole. In salvation we are changed from our previous state to become new creations, persons who are spiritually healthy and who walk in the light, and not in darkness.

God wants everyone to have the opportunity to be saved. He loves every person and does not want anyone to remain outside His offer of salvation. "Indeed God did not send His Son into the world to condemn the world, but in order that the world might be saved through Him" (John 3:17).

Salvation is God's gift to those whom He created in His image and likeness. We need to accept His gift whole-heartedly, treasure it, and share it with others.

My pilgrimage with God

The early Christians were called Followers of the Way. This was the way of life that Jesus had taught. It was "the path" in which they would walk as they made choices of how they would live their lives daily. Walking in Christ's way is not a solitary experience, but a life of relationship and of intimacy with Him through the Holy Spirit that dwells in each believer. It is a life of growth and development. Paul describes it as: "Not that I have already obtained this or have already reached the goal; but I press on to make it my own, because Christ Jesus has made me His own" (Philippians 3:12). We are pressing on in the pilgrimage of life, following the pathway of the Lord.

The Christian life is challenging for the believer. To be able to press on and to grow in the knowledge of Jesus Christ demands the constant commitment of each of us. In chapters 4-6 of Ephesians Paul uses the figure "to walk" to signify "to live." (See these verses in the King James Version.) It the lifestyle or the life pilgrimage of the believer. In each section of these chapters he gives an introduction and a pointed preface to emphasize this point, as seen in the following verses: "I… beg you to lead a life worthy of the calling to which you have been called" (Ephesians 4:2). "Now this I affirm and insist on it in the Lord, you must no longer live as the Gentiles live, in the futility of their minds" (Ephesians 4:17). "Therefore be imitators of God, as beloved children and live in love, as Christ loved us and gave Himself up for us, a fragrant offering and sacrifice to God" (Ephesians 5:1, 2). "Be subject to one another out of reverence for Christ," (Ephesians 5:21). "Finally, be strong in the Lord and in the strength of His mighty power" (Ephesians 6:10).

The Christian life is truly a pilgrimage with God, a life of commitment to Him and His teachings. It's focus and its realization is totally different from that of persons who do not have such a commitment. As we walk with the Lord we know that we are not alone, for His presence continues to point the way.

Helps for the journey

I believe that the greatest help that we have to live our life of commitment to our Lord is **His own presence with us.** "Abide in Me as I abide in you" (John 15:4). We are invited to make our home in Him, as He makes His home in us. A careful and repeated reading of chapters 14-17 of the Gospel of John will help us understand this very personal message that Jesus gave to His disciples, and to us, on the last night of His life prior to the crucifixion. Without a doubt the greatest help we have to live the Christian life is the active presence of Jesus in us through the Holy Spirit which He promised those who love Him and follow His teachings.

It is Christ who taught us to call God Father, and in addition, to do so in the most personal and intimate way, "Abba, Father" (Mark 14:36.) It is a relational name, a name of love that affirms the openness of God to us in any and every situation. In Christ we can experience the constant loving presence of our God with us, guiding us, orienting us, encouraging us, keeping us on track.

Another help for us in our pilgrimage is the **Word of God**, the divine message for God's people, and also a personal message for each pilgrim who walks in God's way. We should love the Bible, meditate on its words, and strive to grow in our knowledge and acceptance of its message.

There are many ways to develop our devotional life. Each of us is different from other persons, and so we should seek the way to read and study God's

Word that is best fitted to help us grow in its truths and its teachings. Insisting that everyone should develop their devotional life in the very same way is to risk frustration in this important aspect of our faith development. We all need to find the best way to develop our reading of God's Word.

The study of the Bible with others in the church setting helps us learn basic truths and enlightening interpretations, and to develop in knowledge of its teachings and how to apply them to our lives. In our private study, reading the Bible aloud and slowly will increase our openness to its message. The use of more than one version or translation of the Bible in our study of specific passages can enhance our understanding of God's message. A good Study Bible with notes can help clarify our understanding of words, cultural differences, historical settings and other relevant matters that are essential for continuing to "grow in knowledge" of God's word.

A good plan for studying the Bible is the inductive method, because it helps us meditate and reflect on its teaching. After reading the passage carefully and slowly you should answer the following questions:

1. What does this passage say?
2. What does this passage want to say (its significance)?
   What did it mean to those to whom it was written?
3. What does this passage mean to me now?

We should never approach reading the Bible as a ritual or as a legalistic requirement, but as a privilege and with anticipation and expectation to see what our loving Heavenly Father wants to say to us.

There are persons who make the Bible their god. For them it is an object of adoration. This was never the intention of God. It is the **Word** of God. In it we find the basic message of God for His people. The psalmist reminds us, "Your word is a lamp to my feet, and a light to my path" (Psalm 119:105). The Bible is holy, but it is God's servant, His word; it is not God, nor is it more than God. We must be careful to avoid an idolatrous relationship with God's word. It is God alone whom we must worship. We must use the Bible as God's word for our growth and development in our spiritual pilgrimage. This is what God wants from us.

Prayer is another important help for the development of our faith and should not be forgotten or neglected. It is an essential in our pilgrimage. Prayer is our conversation with God. Since our Christian faith is relational, we must not ignore the necessity of communion and communication with our God. We must talk with Him, not just in the prayers of our devotional time, or in those in the church, or before meals, but we should do so *constantly.* Our development as Christians depends on this relationship that permits "praying without ceasing." Prayer permits us not only to open ourselves to God, but also to hear His voice and grow in an intimate relationship with Him.

Another help for our journey or pilgrimage is that of **the spiritual gifts** that God gives to each Christian. It is important to know which spiritual gift/s that God has given you and to use them in ways that will bring glory to Him. Spiritual gifts are given by God in the context of the church and find their fulfillment in the ministry of this body. They are given to help us work for the edification and growth of the body of Christ, and to carry out our responsibilities as believers and as witnesses of His presence in our lives.

We should never limit God to the spiritual gifts that are listed in the Bible. God can give the gifts He wishes to His followers. As a Christian woman, you have gifts that God has given you. These have been given to you so that you will use them to bring glory to God and blessing to others. There are times when God will gift you or others for specific "short term" needs in the body of Christ. There are other times when the gift/s will be long-term. When God gifts us, we should seek training so that we may be able to use these gifts in the best way to serve Him.

Another very important help for our spiritual journey is the community God gives us in which we can find significance as individuals, yet, at the same time, be an integral part of a larger relationship. **The church,** the family of God, the body of Christ, is that community. It gives a foundation of significance and support that is essential for the life of faith. One cannot be a Christian alone. We must be in relationship with God through Christ, but in addition we must develop the relationship within the body that is the church to which we belong. This community

Gifts bring glory to God and blessings to others

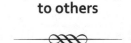

gives us love and acceptance as members of the family of God. It is in this relationship that we are able to grow and develop in our faith. It is in this community that we learn to be responsible and accountable for the use of our spiritual gifts. It is in this community that we press on toward becoming the person God has intended us to become.

These five helps are gifts of God for each of us. He loves us and walks with us in our pilgrimage of faith. The woman who loves Him and wants to walk with Him receives these gifts joyfully and uses them daily.

Signs of the pilgrim

As you read the Gospels you see the many ways in which Jesus walked along the pathways of the land, and "how He went about doing good" (Acts 10:38b). Wherever He went His life was a sign of the power and presence of God. Now, as then, He wants us to be His witnesses and to show signs of our walk with Him, of our pilgrimage of faith. In order that we may do this He has given us a clear understanding of how to develop our lives in an authentic and significant way, so that these signs would be evident for all to witness. For this reason He used words and concepts that are easy for us to understand, yet are profound in their significance and effectiveness.

"You are the **salt of the earth**" (Matthew 5:13a). Just as salt gives savor to food, so the Christian woman should live in such a positive and attractive way as to give savor to her life, the savor of a life that follows the teachings of Christ, making life more meaningful and more significant in every aspect. As salt brings healing to inflammation and infection, the Christian woman should bring healing to others by giving herself to the healing and saving mission of God in the world. As salt produces thirst, she should help others thirst for God as they observe her relationship with Him. The presence of salt, and its function, is mostly unseen, but its effect is notable – in bringing savor to life, in healing, in producing thirst. The lack of salt in one's life means that these positive aspects of its presence will be lacking in the lives of those who need to know of its source, the truth of the message of Christ. Jesus calls us to be salt; this is a sign of the pilgrim.

"You are the **light of the world**" (Matthew 5:14). This ministry is to proclaim in a public and open way the message and the presence of Christ by the way you live. Light should not be placed under a basket, but on a candlestick so that it can lighten the whole house. Light removes darkness and produces new life. Thus the Christian is to be a light for those who walk in darkness. She is to bring light in public and open ways as she shares the good news of Jesus Christ. "…let your light shine before others, so that they may see your good works and give glory to your Father in heaven" (Matthew 5:16). Jesus calls us to be light; this is a sign of the pilgrim.

The Bible also teaches that the follower of Christ is like **yeast**, which serves to leaven the whole mass. (See Luke 13:20-21.) We should be dedicated to producing a more just society, with personal relationships that are more human and humanizing. In order to do so we must live a more transparent and authentic Christian life. Jesus calls us to be yeast, to permeate and bring change to society with His presence and teaching; this is a sign of the pilgrim.

Jesus tells us that we are **His witnesses.** A witness gives testimony of what she has seen or experimented. The Christian woman must learn to say, "For we (I) cannot keep from speaking about what we (I) have seen and heard" (Acts 4:20). To be a witness requires the ability to tell others, without fear, who you are, who Jesus is as your Savior, and what His purpose is for your and their lives. Jesus calls us to be His witnesses; this is a sign of the pilgrim.

Our pilgrimage, as believers, is based on our conversion and our development in the way of our Lord. It is stimulated and helped by God through the active presence of Christ and the Holy Spirit in our lives, through the reading of the Bible, prayer, spiritual gifts, and the Christian community to which we belong. In response we, as Christians, accept as ours these "signs of the pilgrim," to be salt, light, yeast, and a faithful witness of Christ Jesus. Each of these will continue to stimulate our spiritual development and should be used conscientiously in our daily lives, which is our pilgrimage with our Lord.

My spiritual development

Our growth and development is a reality of life. Not only do women develop from one stage to another in their chronological and social life, but also in their spiritual life. Paul speaks of Christians who are still children and who are not ready for solid food and must still be given milk to drink (I Corinthians 3:2). We need to stop being children and grow "in the grace and knowledge of our Lord and Savior Jesus Christ" (2 Peter 3:18).

To be a Christian woman demands that we take an honest look at where we are in our spiritual development and in our pilgrimage. Is your faith rigid? Is it truly yours? Is your faith one of works? Are you able to overcome the doubts and the incongruities of your life? Have you been able to reflect on your faith and come to basic and fundamental conclusions that are truly yours? Is your commitment to Christ authentic and does it influence every aspect of your life? These are but a few of the essential questions the Christian woman in her life pilgrimage needs to ask and seek to answer.

The following spiritual goals may stimulate your development as a woman of faith. Each one calls you to become aware of the stage of your present development as well as to challenge you to continue growing in your faith:

1. Recognize the reality and complexity of your holistic development: physical, mental, emotional, and spiritual. Determine different ways to evaluate your development in each of these areas.

2. Accept your own responsibility for your development as a child of God, and help others who are progressing in their faith development. Our interdependence as the body of Christ is a most important factor in our faith development as individuals and as a group.

3. Learn to share your story, your testimony, with others. Recognize it as an integral part of the story of the God's people. Sharing your testimony with others in a truthful and transparent way will not only strengthen your spiritual development but help others in theirs.

4. Develop the ability to reflect on the significance of your faith, of your beliefs, and of authentic ways in which you express your faith daily.

5. Develop the ability to relate honestly and caringly with others as you speak the truth in love. This is a step toward constructing confidence one in another, and thus promoting growth and relationship.

6. Understand that your role as a believer is to minister in God's name. As you develop spiritually the doors of service and ministry will open more widely and will expand toward new horizons of participation in the Kingdom of God.

7. Analyze the social factors that fight against our faith in today's world. Recognize their noxious influence and formulate a conscientious position of ways to limit their influence in your life and in the life of your church and community. Find ways to do so that would be pleasing to Christ.

8. Develop tolerance for the ambiguities or incongruities of daily life. A person without this capacity will become frustrated and stagnated in the faith or will become rigid in the way in which they face the realities of life, and thus limit their positive influence in the lives of others.

9. Learn to be hopeful and to give hope to others. Peter, in times of crisis, speaks of a *living hope* into which we have been born anew through the resurrection of Jesus Christ (1 Peter 1:3).

My faith began with my salvation experience. It grows as I continue in my pilgrimage with Christ, and as I recognize and use the helps that God gives me: His active presence, His Word, communion with Him in prayer, spiritual gifts and participation in His church, the Christian community. I respond to these great gifts with the signs of the pilgrim, becoming salt, light, yeast and an authentic witness of my Lord.

My spiritual development is a great challenge. It is a task for my entire life. As a Christian woman with an intimate relationship with God, I am growing from one stage of Christian development to another, conscious of the grace of God that works in me. I acknowledge that I am special in God's eyes and thus I will respond to His love in increasingly authentic ways that will reflect my growth and development as a Christian woman.

Activities for reflection and learning

1. Write a history of your own spiritual pilgrimage. It can include experiences of your childhood, your youth, your conversion and your spiritual development. Analyze where you are now and your need for growth. As a result of this study and your reflection on it, do you need to make a decision about how to move forward in your spiritual development? If so, what are the steps you will take?

2. Make a list of the principle values you believe in. Prioritize them with the first being the most important. How do these values influence your spiritual development? Are there others that should be added at this particular moment in your pilgrimage? Are you willing to do so?

3. Select a hymn that expresses well what you feel about your development as a Christian. Sing it. It would be well to memorize it so that it could continue to affirm or challenge your spiritual development at any time.

Questions to answer alone or in a group

• What does it mean to you to be saved? Is there a specific personal anecdote that helps you to express what you feel about your experience with the Lord?

• Do you feel that you have grown spiritually in the past three months? How?

• How does Christ help you on your spiritual pilgrimage? Give specific examples.

- Which of the spiritual goals presented in this chapter will help you most in your Christian development? Why? Are there other goals that you would add? If so, how can you implement them?

4. As a Person Different from Men

"The truly capable woman – who can find her?
She if far beyond the price of pearls.
When she opens her mouth, she does so wisely:
On her tongue is kindly instruction.
Her children stand up and proclaim her blessed,
Her husband, too, sings her praises."
Proverbs 31:10, 26, 28 NJB

W ho is woman? Who is man? How can we understand ourselves better? How can we experience and develop the potential the Lord has given us as His special creation? How can I become the woman that I should be? These and other questions fill our minds as we try to understand ourselves and our relationship with the opposite sex more clearly. But first, who are we as women?

On many occasions as women we experience rejection or marginalization from society simply because we are women. Data compiled during the International Decade of Women (1976-1986) indicates that while women are approximately fifty percent of the world's population, they do two-thirds of the work, earn a tenth part of the profit, and are owners of less that one percent of the world's total property. These statistics have not changed that much in the ensuing years.

According to *The Penguin Atlas of Women in the World*[7] in 2009, of the nearly one billion illiterates worldwide, about two-thirds are women. 1.2 billion of the world's people subsist on only $1 a day and an estimated seven out of ten of the world's hungry are women and girls. The lack of safe water and sanitation is the world's single largest cause of illness. More than one billion people lack access to improved water supply. Women and girls, as the "water haulers" for their families, walk on an average six kilometers a day, carrying 20 liters of water. As girls reach puberty they often have to leave school to help carry water for their families. International organizations are recognizing that when the mother and girls are educated the health and the economy of the family are greatly improved. As a result more and more emphasis is being given to education for girls, such as in the Millennium Development Goals (See Appendix A). Already it is seen that the children of women with five years of primary education are 40 percent more likely to live beyond the age of five.

The global population of refugees including internally displaced people is estimated at between 35 and 45 million. Women's responsibility for caring for their families is increased in these settings where there are fewer resources available for them to meet their needs.

Women's bodies are commodities in the global sex trade, a multi-billion dollar industry. As a result of the AIDS/HIV epidemic there is an increasing demand for younger girls as "safe" commercial sex partners. Over 30 million adults in the world are HIV infected, seventy percent of whom live in Sub-Saharan Africa. More than half of this number are women. Most will die due to the lack of medical treatment. Women, the traditional caretakers of families, often have no one to care for them when they are ill. Their deaths leave households without support. There is an estimated population of 15 million AIDS orphans worldwide. Orphaned girls are particularly vulnerable to sexual and economic exploitation and as a result to HIV infection.

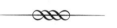

7 out of 10 of the world's hungry are women and girls

"In its first study of women's health around the globe, the World Health Organization said that the AIDS virus is the leading cause of death and disease among women between the ages of 15 and 44. Unsafe sex is the leading risk factor in developing countries for these women of childbearing age, the WHO said. The data were included in a report that attempts to highlight the unequal health treatment a female faces from childbirth into maturity and old age."[8]

For millions of women, the home is the most dangerous place they could be. Women suffer cruelties and violence in their homes every day. Domestic violence is the most ubiquitous constant in women's lives around the world.

Each year about 200 million women become pregnant. Over half a million of these will die as a result. Another 50 million will suffer long-term disability or illness as a consequence of pregnancy and childbirth. Africa has the lowest life expectancy for women.

The majority of the world's women do not equally own, inherit or control property, land and wealth. Globalization has tended to deepen women's property disadvantage as a cash economy has displaced communal or household-based land use.

Women only own one hundredth of world property, and are earners of one-tenth of world income.

Seeing this sad truth in our world today, we become discouraged. How many times a girl, and later when she is a woman, will say, "Oh, if only I were a man," because she recognizes that there are differences in opportunity, in prestige, in social status, in remuneration, in responsibility and in realizations for men and for women. Depending on the personal development of the woman affected by this situation, her response may be resignation or it may be rebellion. Other women may consider themselves to be caught in the middle, not treated as a woman or as a sexual person, but rather as one of neuter gender, another form and extension of a "non-person". Others may feel that they are marginalized, deprived, treated as an object or a "thing," and all the while feeling guilty about these thoughts!

But there are women who reflect seriously about their lives and those of others. They search for ways of truly becoming human and of living in such a way as to promote the humanity of other women as well as the humanity of their male counterparts. As Christian women this should be our response and our commitment. We must remember that we both, male and female, are made in God's image and likeness. We are distinct from men, but we are neither inferior nor superior to them. It is of great importance that we recognize these differences as we press toward becoming all that God has desired us to be.

Woman - her place

There are very contradictory positions about women in today's world. On Mothers' Day it seems that she is the most idealized and respected person in the world, but when she "finds her voice" and speaks of occupying some non-traditional position, immediately she hears voices that totally reject that possibility, "because she is a woman," she must be kept "in her place." It is sad to note that sometimes it is the same voice that takes such contradictory positions. And, sadder still that often it has been other Christian women who take a stand against the progress of women.

Truthfully it is difficult to speak of the role of women without exaggeration from one side or the other. There are those who insist that woman is inferior to man. She is his servant, his slave. And there are those who insist that woman is equal to man and thus is in competition with him. But there are also those who insist that woman is superior to man, in sentiments, in abilities, in potential, and thus seeks to take his place in social and public life.

I believe these attempts to find the true identity of women to be totally wrong. One can appreciate positions taken by each, and as women we can understand the reactions of the women who have taken the last two positions, because many times we have experienced circumstances where we have not only not been understood, but we have been oppressed. Unfortunately this experience is found in the family, in the educational system, in the workplace, in the community, and in the church.

It is not my purpose here to present this aspect of women's reality as a "consciousness taking" event because I believe that the majority of women have already experienced these realities and are aware of this situation. If we haven't, it is because we do not want to recognize it or the cultural blinders we wear are so strong that we are conditioned to not recognize these truths. My purpose is to help us know who we truly are as Christian women. We have emphasized earlier that women are human beings, made in God's image. We are special! We are of incalculable value.

The search for women's identity is not new in our times; it is found in the history of many cultures. In our Judeo-Christian tradition we must recognize that a very strong prejudice toward women has developed over the centuries. For example, Rabbi Ben Sira in the apocryphal book of *Ecclesiastes* said, "Sin began with a woman, and thanks to her we all must die" (25:24.) When Jesus was born the social and religious norms had been established: women were isolated and kept in their place. She could not talk in public; she could not take care of her own affairs; she was inferior socially, religiously, and politically. During the different stages of her life she was considered to be the possession of either her father, her husband, or her son. Jewish men prayed, giving thanks to God, "Oh, God, I thank you that I was not born a Gentile, a slave, or a woman."

In such a setting, Jesus was born. He came in to the world through the body of a pious young woman. This woman found her destiny and her identity through this experience in which she was willing to do the will of God (Luke 1:38). When Jesus began His ministry He knew that His responsibility was to minister to both women and men, and in doing so, He liberated both. He was not limited by the norms of His day, nor the laws, the customs, nor the accepted prejudices of society. He talked with women, He healed them, He made them whole, and He inspired them to follow Him and to give their lives in His service.

Luke 8:1-3 says that Jesus traveled from place to place with His disciples, including women who had been cured of evil spirits and diseases. These women were helping to support the group out of their own resources! No rabbi or any other leader had women in their following, for women couldn't study, they couldn't give their opinion on anything, they couldn't even talk to a man. But the Gospels emphasize the special relationship that Jesus had with women: the Samaritan woman, Martha and Mary, Mary Magdalene, Susana and Juana, among others. Not only were they His friends, they were His disciples. They learned from Him and He considered them worthy to be with Him in His kingdom work, to learn and discuss theological matters, to know new realities of their relationship with the Heavenly Father.

A careful reading of Luke 10:38-42 and John 11:1-12:8 reveals much about the relationship between Jesus and the family at Bethany. In one of His visits Mary took the position of a student when she sat at His feet to listen to His teachings, and in the context of the death and burial of Lazarus, Martha has one of the most profound theological discussions with Jesus found in the Gospels. Jesus included women in His ministry then, and He continues to do so today!

So, you and I need to affirm our value and our identity as women created in the image of God. Again, our identity has its foundation in God and as a result our potential for growth is unlimited. In addition, Christ, our Savior, has liberated us from the prejudices and enslaving bonds handed down through the years, giving us in their place freedom from bondage, and abundant life.

Remember the words of Jesus, "If you continue in My word, you are really My disciples, and you will know the truth and the truth will make you free.... So, if the Son makes you free, you will be free indeed" (John 8:31, 32 and 36). What is woman's place in the world? In the family? In the church? Woman's place is in the liberating plan of Christ! We do not have to enslave ourselves to ideas that are far from those of our Lord, nor allow others to do so to us. We can be free indeed!

Woman, different from man

Psychology continues to help us in our understanding of human personality, but there are fundamental studies that still present a very biased view of the role of women. Most psychological investigation has been based on studies of the male population, but the results of these studies have been used for both men and women. As a result, values that are considered in the development of human personality are specific to the values of men, but these same values and their corresponding developmental tasks have been considered normative for women also.

Sigmund Freud, the famed psychoanalyst whose writings have been so influential, considered women to be inferior to men, anxious, nervous and envious because she was not like him. In addition he taught that women showed less sense of justice than men; that they were less apt to meet the challenges of the great demands of life; and that women's feelings of affection or hostility influenced her decisions more frequently. Other influential psychologists and psychiatrists have followed in this same trend in the past decades. Their conclusions have been that women are not only different from men and make decisions differently from them, but, it would seem, that they are "less than normal."

Today there are many in the field of Psychology and Psychiatry who are doing more detailed studies of the Psychology of Women. There are many books that have been published about women's identity, her development, her potential and every aspect of her life. A most interesting book about the psychology of women was written by Carol Gilligan,[9] professor of education at the University of Harvard, called *In a Different Voice*. She, along with many other modern psychologists and sociologists, affirm that men and women are different, and that each has a different perspective about their lives and about their relationships. Women are oriented toward life with a sense of responsibility toward their relationships, especially when these relationships are with persons of significance. Women also have a sense of attachment and affiliation that colors her relationships.

Men have a different orientation toward life. They are more positional, they relate more to the circumstances and to the rights of the individual. Even in the sexual lives of men and women their perspectives tend to be different. In an interesting investigation of the projective imagination among the sexes, the fantasy of men was of strength while that of women was of care.

Studies done in Developmental Psychology conclude that the following values are important for healthy adulthood: autonomy, separation from one's parents, to be one's self, to be an authentic person, to develop one's individuality, and the appropriation of the natural rights of the individual.

These are all aspects of the masculine focus toward life and relationship.

There is a pressing need to recognize that women find their sense of personhood in a different way: through making and maintaining affiliations and relationships. The total psychic structure of women is based on her potential to be more connected, more related to others. She rejects, or wants to reject, aggression as a form of life. But when our society teaches that women have to be like men to be "normal," that she must be more aggressive, more assertive, more autonomous, more positional, it is at this point where her problems begin. Psychologically she is trying to be who she is not. Society needs to begin to value the perspective of women as much as that of men. Then the freedom for healthy development of each will find its true realization. Life will have more meaning; the relationship between man and woman will be more meaningful, and more in accord with the original plan of the Creator when He made us different.

Allow me a brief parenthesis at this moment. Women who feel so responsible for others many times do not sense any responsibility toward themselves. If she thinks of her own needs, she and others will call her "self-centered," "egotistical," or "selfish." If she thinks of her own survival or in taking care of herself, immediately she condemns herself for doing so. Women have been programmed from birth that their role is that of self-sacrifice in everything. It seems that it is in our DNA.

Loving ourselves is a healthy part of being able to love God and others.

However, we must remember that if we are not responsible and careful to care for ourselves, we will be unable to relate well to others. We need to love ourselves, to take time for ourselves, to care for and to help ourselves. If we are careful to do this we will have something of worth to share with others: a firm and healthy foundation for relating with others. It is important to remember that when Jesus was questioned about which was the greatest commandment, He responded, "'You shall love the Lord your God with all your heart, and with all your soul, and with all your mind.' This is the greatest and first commandment. And a second is like it: 'You shall love your neighbor as yourself.' On these two commandments hang all the law and the prophets." (Matthew 22:37-39). Loving ourselves is a healthy part of being able to love God and others.

In 1848 there was a women's congress in the State of New York where they were to consider the social, civil, and religious condition of women and their rights in these areas. One of those attending, Elizabeth Cody Stanton, inflamed because of the restrictions on women, boldly said to a reporter there, "put it down in capital letters, self-development is a higher duty than self-sacrifice. The thing which most retards and militates against women's self-development is self-sacrifice."[10] Self-sacrifice without a strong sense of purpose weakens women and probably enslaves those for whom she sacrifices herself.

We should acknowledge the fact that women have the responsibility to consider themselves and their needs as much as they consider others. From a theological position we need to remember that both the Old and New Testaments speak of the importance of loving others as much as we love ourselves (Leviticus 19:18b and Matthew 23:34-40). Dr. Jean Miller, a psychoanalyst and specialist in women's psychology, says that we must have a new Psychology of Women and that it must begin from a different perspective: that of women's own development. This psychology must be based on the following concepts:

1. "Women stay with, build on, and develop in a context of attachment and affiliation with others.

2. Women's sense of self becomes very much organized around being able to make, and then to maintain, affiliations and relationships.

3. For many women, the threat of disruption of an affiliation is perceived not just as a loss of a relationship but as something closer to a total loss of self."[11]

Without a doubt this is a different voice advocating for the formation of a psychology of women's life centered in the possibility of a totally distinct approach, one that is more significant and more appreciative of women's interests and values; a psychology of women in which affiliation is affirmed more than the traditional traits or values of autonomy and individualization.

In order to become the special woman we can be, we must understand more fully who we are and what the psychological emphases of our lives are. Studies such as these will open the way to the possibility of constructing a Psychology of Women that truly reflects the perspective of women, and of her daily life as an adult.

Today in almost any university in any area of the world there is a Department of Women's Studies where new psychological systems are studied and investigations are carried on in the area of women's interests and development. As a result many women are affirming the progress made by their gender and are entering into both traditional and non-traditional professional roles with a greater appreciation for their personhood. Women occupy the presidency in some countries. They are found in every profession - governors, lawyers, senators, professors, teachers, doctors, nurses, pastors, engineers, architects, artists, writers, and many more. At the same time in some areas of the world women continue to be oppressed and limited in their personal freedom. As Christian women we can pray for these women and become an advocate for freedom and justice everywhere.

Man and woman: both human beings, and partners

In her book, *Identity,* Ruth Tiffany Barnhouse,[12] a Christian Psychiatrist and a seminary professor, says that it is difficult for women to find their own identity because there are so many stereotypical identities that have been given to both men and women. Not only are these stereotypes limiting, but they are also harmful to both sexes and to their relationships. We are not all equal and when we try to say that we are, we traumatize our lives and those of others. There are many facets of our identity: gender, age, maturity, mental and physical health, intelligence, nationality, culture, and temperament, among others. Psychological factors such as being introverted or extroverted, logical or sentimental, intuitive or practical are all basic elements in the formation of the identity of persons.

Men and women are different in the ways in which they orient and develop their lives, and each man or woman is distinct from every other man or woman. There are tragic consequences when we try to force ourselves or others to fit into a preconceived or stereotypical mold. However, we need to recognize that there are certain basic characteristics that are found more frequently in men or in women.

Men tend to look at moral problems in an analytical way: dividing the problem into parts and then choosing the more precise or correct part as the solution. On the other hand women tend to look at the whole picture, including the relationships involved, thus making it more difficult for her to make a decision. Men tend to be more oriented toward specific goals while women tend to look at situations and relationships. The voice of both genders should be heard, because both perspectives are needed for more balanced and healthy decisions.

For the good of humanity there must be mutual respect between men and women. Each of them must learn to acknowledge and appreciate the differences in their perspectives and they must know, appreciate and cultivate the elements of their shared humanity As human beings they have mutual goals, even though as men and women they may be very different one from another in their way of approaching these goals.

We must learn how not to allow these differences to be a source of contention between us, but to appreciate the fullness of our complementarity. In this way men and women can do together more than the sum of what they can do apart.

The woman who knows well who she is and is conscious and healthfully proud of her talents and abilities, knowing how and when to use them for the good of all in the relationship, is in a position to be effective in bringing about the change needed to do away with the imbalance between men and women in all aspects of their lives. Women should have confidence in themselves and in the validity of their understanding of life: how they see it and how they interpret it. They should be able to present and defend their interpretation and their decisions with an assured firmness based on their own development as women created in the image of God. In this moment, and only then, it will be possible to experience the liberation of the totality of humanity, because men are not truly free until women are free.

Feminism, by trying to place men in a position of inequality and disregard as well as those persons who have seen men as enemy are both wrong. One, as much as the other, produces a lamentable situation. We must emphasize what we have in common; we must be allies, companions in our common search for our own humanity. Both men and women are companions and partners in this pilgrimage.

Women are special, and are different from men. She will find a greater personal significance when she acknowledges that God has made her in this way. Also that it is her Creator's plan that she find, along with men, this special relationship that will allow each of them to treat the other with mutual appreciation and respect, recognizing the special qualities of the other. In this way they both become co-heirs of the plan of God for His creation.

I'm a woman! I'm special! I'm special in my relationship with men. I bring to these relationships my special point of view and the importance I give to relating with others. When I follow this perspective, I am faithful to who I am, faithful to my partner, and faithful to God and the plan He has for my life. In such a setting God can bless my life and my relationships not only my own personal experience, but also the lives of all those with whom I relate in the different areas of my life.

Activities for reflection and learning

1. Describe how you and a man (husband, father, son, uncle, grandfather, etc.) resolve a crisis in your family. Reflect on the differences between your way of thinking and acting with men's way. How do you feel about this situation? Is the way you resolve a crisis given equal value to the way a man resolves it? If there is a difference, how do you feel about it? What will you do about it?

2. Why do you think that God made man and woman so different? Explain how our differences help us come together and give more significance to our lives.

3. Using both Luke 19:2-10 and John 8:1-11 reflect on the value of the person as an individual as seen in these texts. Give special attention to the idea of the person and their self-concept before and after their encounter with Christ. Do you note a change that the person has of him/herself after having their lives changed by Christ? What are those changes? As a Christian woman, what can you learn from the teachings of these passages for changes in your own life?

Questions to answer alone or in a group

- What does it mean to be a woman?

- Do you like being a woman, or would you prefer to be a man? Why?

- What can we do to promote true companionship between men and women? Are you willing to do this?

- Name ways in which Jesus affirmed the values He saw in both men and women.

  Does He continue to do so today? How?

5. As a Wife

> And Jesus said, "Have you not read that the One who
> made them at the beginning 'made them male and female'
> and said, "For this reason a man shall leave his father
> and mother and be joined to his wife, and the two shall
> become one flesh'? So they are no longer two, but one
> flesh. Therefore what God has joined together,
> let no one separate." Matthew 19:4-6

As we have seen, to be a woman is to be special. When women know who they are and how to develop their identity in a wise way, and men recognize who they are and how to develop their identity adequately, and both of them seek mutual satisfaction and realization, there is a great potential for their mutual happiness. Unfortunately even in our churches we have not been prepared for this life of mutuality, of love, of giving of oneself to the other, for this life of significance. However, the church is the best place to learn these truths, because they come from the plan of God for His creation – for both men and women - from the very beginning. As you read these pages and reflect on them you should experience a new appreciation of these truths; you should come to feel that "I'm a woman! I'm special! I am a person who is searching for my identity as a human being, hoping to relate in love and respect with others."

In the last chapter we have considered the differences that exist between men and women, differences designed and brought into being by our Heavenly Father, differences that accentuate the possibility of mutuality, of reciprocity, of complementarity, of happiness. Now we need to think about what the Bible teaches about women as wives.

Woman, a help-meet ... equal to him
- Genesis 2:18, 20, 23

In chapter 2 of Genesis we see the development of creation in a very personal way, with God involving Himself very intimately in the development of His creation, especially the human race. In contrast with the majesty of Genesis 1, we see God solicitous about Adam, molding him from the earth, giving him the breath of life, placing him in the garden, giving him responsibilities and limits, forming a help-meet for him, one like him and made from the mutual essence of creation. This passage speaks of the unity of man and woman, of their companionship, their mutual relationship, their reciprocity.

We hear the immortal words of God, "It is not good for man to be alone" (Genesis 2:18). The word "help-meet" in Hebrew means "a helper that corresponds to him" or "a helper who is before him." There is a mutual relationship, a great affinity; they have a mutual task to fulfill: to eliminate the loneliness of each other, to work together caring for the garden, and to be companion or partner one to the other in all aspects of life.

When God brings the woman to Adam he receives her with enthusiasm and joy, "This is it!" are the joyous words of man. There is a special union between the two: they are formed from the same body – flesh and bones. Without a doubt the happiness Adam expresses must have been felt by the woman also. How wonderful it must have been to be together, to talk, to share ideas, to love one another and to share mutual experiences.

Both men and women are help-meets one to the other. This ability to help the other should not be considered as an example of weakness nor of inferiority. The Bible frequently speaks of God as our help or our helper. When we are a helper, a help-meet, we help the other from who we are, not just from our strengths, but also from our weaknesses, and from our distinct perspective. One helps the one he/she loves from the totality of who he/she is. We cannot separate the help that is given from our identity as a man or woman. When we deny help to the other from our identity as a man or woman, we sin and we become less that what God wanted for us, even from Creation.

Even though we must not leave to one side the importance of our mutual need of a "help-meet," in which both man and woman are the precise "help-meet" the other needs, now we want to look at how we, women and wives, can become help-meets. I want to share with you three biblical ideas that expand on this concept.

1. "The virtuous wife" - Proverbs 31:10-31

Many of the proverbs speak of women, some positively, but others show the very low concept of women held by the Hebrew people at the time in which these proverbs were being compiled. It is not necessary to call attention to these negative passages in this moment, only to recognize that Jewish women, and we ourselves in consequence, have been influenced by these negative considerations that, in many ways, have been taken as normative.

The traditional Jew reads Proverbs 31:10-31 to his wife and children every Friday evening in the Sabbath observance in the home. This time was the most sacred time of the week when the whole family gathered together reverently to remember their history, to affirm their identity as a covenant people, and their responsibility before God and the community. Can you imagine the impact that hearing this passage read and affirmed fifty-two times a year would have on the identity of Jewish women? When I think of this reality it is not surprising that the Jewish family has survived and prospered. Read this passage and you will easily recognize how its repetition in such a sacred context would impact the goals set by the Jewish woman for her role in life.

This passage is an acrostic. Its form helped its readers to remember it more easily and at the same time it shows the effort that the writer had taken to give a holistic view (the whole picture) of the virtuous woman, a good wife.

Using this passage as a model commentary on the virtuous woman we can emphasize the following distinct qualities:

- **Faithful** (v. 11.) "The heart of her husband trusts in her, and he will have no lack of gain." She is a good housewife; she knows how to manage money well and does not waste it. But I like to think that her husband can have confidence in her in other things: her activities, her thoughts, her loyalty as a mother, wife and citizen, and in her values or ideals. In everything her husband can trust her.

- **Considerate** (v. 12.) "She does him good and not harm all the days of her life." We know that frequently this is not true, but rather just the opposite. Women can do harm and not good to their husbands by her actions that stem from resentment or suppressed feelings of inferiority.

Knowing our husbands well we have the possibility of doing him harm, mistreating or destroying his personality because we know his weak points. Instead of helping him and being considerate of him, we can harm him. The virtuous woman does not react in this way, she is considerate of her husband, she "does him good and not harm" daily. She will have his interests and needs in mind in all her actions.

- **Worker** (vv. 13 cf.) It seems that this quality is over-emphasized in this passage. Jewish women were central to the well-run household in biblical times, but it seems that this woman works too much. She "works with willing hands," "she rises while it is still night and provides food for her household," "she considers a field and buys it with the fruit of her hands she plants a vineyard," "her lamp does not go out at night," "she puts her hands to the distaff," "she makes linen garments and sells them," "she looks well to the ways of her household and does not eat the bread of idleness!"

Truthfully, I get tired just reading this passage. Nevertheless I believe that many Christian and Jewish women think, "this is the way it is." The virtuous woman portrayed here is a good worker, but she is larger than life and certainly no woman could do all that is listed here in a single day. If it were not for the other qualities that are more "human," we might think that she was nothing more than a very effective "machine," a slave to her role as a homemaker.

Work is not punishment meted out by God

Sometimes people think that work was the punishment meted out by God in the Garden of Eden, however this is not so. From the very beginning God gave the first couple the task of working and caring for the garden. Nevertheless, we must recognize that whether it be a man or a woman forced labor that overburdens a person can embitter and weaken anyone, and make life impossible for them. Everyone should have a healthy ratio of work and rest. Our bodies are part of God's creation and we are responsible for caring for them.

- **Shares with others** (v. 20) The virtuous woman does not hoard her wealth nor consider that since she is such a hard worker and has been privileged to be successful in her efforts, that everyone else should "work hard like I do." She extends her hand to the poor! She is compassionate and humble and follows the leading of God in caring for the needs of the underprivileged and disadvantaged in her community.

In "opening her hand to the poor and reaching out her hands to the needy" she helps us see the way in which help can be given to others in a respectful way. In extending her hand she is not giving a "hand out," but a "hand up," thus helping to maintain the dignity of the person in need. This is one of the most beautiful expressions of a woman who identifies with the community, is saddened by the conditions of the poor and does what she can to change that situation and hopefully to change the society that has produced it.

- **Not afraid of the future** (v. 21.) She is not paralyzed with fear of tomorrow. She knows that she is constantly preparing herself for whatever eventuality might occur, and so she is not enslaved by fear. She does not think about all the negative things that can occur in her life or in that of her family, such as a snowstorm, for instance. She has made provision beforehand and therefore can handle the crisis.

- **Teaches with wisdom and kindness** (v. 26.) She is not a rigid person in her responsibility with her children and with her husband. She is wise, but at the same time she is tolerant and kind. As a result her children, her husband, and even the elders who meet in the gates of the city, praise her for who she is. What a wonderful gift to give to others, words that are both wise and kind. These qualities make her a true "help-meet" to her family and to others.

- **Virtuous** (vv. 10, 25, and 30.) The virtues in these three verses are seen also in the whole passage. "She is far more precious than jewels," "strength and dignity are her clothing," Her "fear of the Lord" and her positive relationship with Him is like a crown that secures and culminates her virtuous character.

What do you think of this virtuous woman? She is an excellent example of what the Jewish community considered as a help-meet, "the suitable partner" who had been created by God. She is a good example for us today, also.

2. Love: The more excellent way
- 1 Corinthians 12:31-13:13

The second idea that I want to emphasize for women, the "suitable partner," is love. It is interesting that in the passage in Proverbs love is not mentioned.

It does not mean that love is not important. Physical love was important for the Jew and is expressed beautifully in the Song of Songs that praises this relationship of joy and companionship. It is a good book for couples to read together to help them respond to this important part of their married life.

The Bible speaks a great deal of love: the love of God for His creation, His love in sending His Son to be our Savior, the love of Christ shown in His ministry and in His sacrifice. In addition there are three great chapters of the Bible that speak of love: Hosea 11; 1 Corinthians 13 and 1 John 4. Read all three carefully in order to reflect on their words and as a stimulus for you and your husband in your search for the teachings on love in the Bible.

How can a healthy and meaningful love relationship help us become "a help-meet," "a suitable partner," to our husbands? There are qualities of love that are found in these three chapters that both husband and wife can incorporate in our lives. Here, however, I will limit our attention to those found in Paul's letter to the Corinthians in verses 4-7.

> "Love is patient,
> Love is kind;
> Love is not envious or boastful or arrogant or rude;
> Love does not insist on its own way;
> Love is not irritable or resentful;
> Love does not rejoice in wrongdoing, but rejoices in truth.
> Love bears all things,
> Love believes all things;
> Love hopes all things;
> Love endures all things.
> Love never ends."

A good exercise to help you grow in your love one for another is to grade yourself on each of these characteristics. As a result of your conclusions make the decision to improve in those areas where you are weakest. Be sure to make specific goals. Don't try to do it all at once, but take one characteristic at a time, spending a week on each to try to improve that specific characteristic. Then you can begin on another one, and you will see how you will "grow in love" in the more excellent way.

This passage helps us consider the characteristics of true love, to recognize that without love we are nothing as Paul emphasizes in the first verses of this chapter. Recognizing how difficult it is to incorporate all of these qualities of love in our daily experience, I would like to direct your attention to the passage in 1 John 4: *"God is love, and love comes from God."* God helps us, both men and women, to grow in love, to be more loving, to know how to love. What a wonderful helper we have to show us the way!

Psychoanalyst Eric Fromm in his book *The Art of Love*[13], gives two teachings that I think are very relevant to our study. He says that there are certain basic elements in love: care, respect, responsibility and knowledge. The one who loves knows, respects, cares for, and feels responsibility for the one who is loved. These elements are mutually interdependent and are found in a mature person. And just as importantly, the one who does not know, does not respect, does not care for, nor feel responsible for the one loved, does not love. In such a setting love does not exist.

Fromm also says that when one loves another, they seek the happiness and development of the other person. When we love our husbands we seek not only their happiness, but also their development as men, as our husbands and as fellow human beings. In turn, when our husbands love us, they seek our happiness and our development as women, as their wives, and as fellow human beings.

I believe that these two concepts are indispensable for us to become a true "helpmeet," a person that truly loves another.

3. The true "help-meet"

As mentioned previously, sometimes we think that being a "help-meet" to our husbands means that we are his slave, to do his will. Others consider that it will mean being his protector, a "mother" who protects him from all his faults, perpetuating his lack of responsibility. To accept either of these roles as the true meaning of "help-meet" is an ill-conceived use of our capacity to help and care for another person, in this case our husbands. In carrying out such unsound practices we do not allow him to grow in his own responsibility as a human being. Many women spend their entire lives protecting the ego of their husbands, covering up their faults and hiding their weaknesses, so that others will see them in a positive light. As a result men will think that someone is going to cover his tracks all his life: his mother, his wife, his secretary, his co-worker, his daughter. It is a vicious cycle in which all are diminished; all are "less that human." Nevertheless, there are many women who do this all their lives. However, if you are going to be a "help-meet" to your husband, you must help him in ways in which he can be who he really is, can grow and be responsible in his actions. The same can be said for the way in which a husband can be a "help-meet" to his wife, helping her be authentic to who she is and responsible in her actions. Being a "help-meet" is a truly humanizing and loving experience. The couple who live in such a relationship are truly blessed.

One flesh - Genesis 2:24

The writer of Genesis has a good understanding of what it means to "not be alone." It is to unite with another and become "one flesh." Without a doubt this refers to sexual relations. This most intimate relation should be one that unifies the couple; that signifies companionship instead of loneliness and signifies love and consideration as well as sexual desire. There should be a sense of companionship that emphasizes the idea that the sexual act is a symbolic act of the relationship in all areas of life, in the way in which the two encounter significance and companionship in the distinct areas of their shared experiences.

But being one flesh signifies more than the sexual relation. It signifies becoming a married couple, coming to have a married identity, being "the Smiths," (Put your name there) becoming "us." Truthfully this "us" is more than the sum of the two parts; it is more than "him and me," because the relationship itself begins to have an additional significance: the two become "one flesh."

It is easy to understand the importance of this effort toward becoming "one flesh." If the two partners of this relationship are not in accord, if there is a constant battle between them, if there is no comprehension and willingness to work together, it will be very difficult for them to become one, to become "we" and "us." There must be a willingness, a desire, a constant effort, before the marriage and afterwards to experience this special relationship. Becoming "one flesh" is not attained in a single day or in a single act; it is a lifelong task. It is a process that will demand our constant attention and dedication throughout the marriage.

There are those who think that "one flesh" is simply a way of incorporating the personality of one partner into the personality of the other, and in this way of thinking it would be that of the woman being incorporated into her husband's personality, since traditionally she is seen as the person of less value. This is not biblical in any sense of the word. Unfortunately, however, there are women who are afraid to have or to share any idea or position that is not that of her husband. She is like his shadow; again a "non-person."

The good news of the Bible is its emphasis on the value of each person made in God's image - valued for their ability to think, to speak, to question, to make decisions, and to relate to others. The two persons who form the married couple and who have these characteristics come together to form "one flesh". This cannot be something that is forced on them or something they pretend to be. It is a giving of oneself, a desire, a willingness on the part of each to work together to become one, known together as a couple.

Modern Psychology helps us understand the importance of maintaining equilibrium between the sense of unity of the couple and the sense of being two separate individuals. In order to have a healthy and balanced life each one needs to be an individual who knows who she/he is and how they should develop their lives. At the same time, they must be persons who are able to relate to others, and want to do so. Probably the number one problem in the marriage is that of not resolving the necessity of maintaining that healthy equilibrium between the sense of unity of the couple, and the sense of individuality of each partner. "One flesh" does not mean to do away with the individuality of the person, it means a healthy balance between being a couple and at the same time being two individuals.

Some women have felt that they cannot develop the gifts or capacities that God has given them because they will have trouble with their husbands by doing something that he does not do, or by doing something better than he does. How many women have not developed their gifts thinking that this would be contrary to the will of God. How wrong they are! They have limited the blessings of God for themselves, for their families, for their church and for the community in which they live because of this misguided abandonment of their God-given abilities.

Being "one flesh" is feeling united in body and soul, in interests and in effort, in working together toward the building of the relationship and of the significance of becoming a couple. However, it is not and never should be the destruction of the personality of one or the other of the two persons. Each one should see that their personality, their own sense of personhood, is developed even more in marriage. Being "one flesh" should produce a sense of realization for each partner. The happiness of each person is essential for this reality to come to fulfillment. In becoming "one flesh" each one thinks, expresses him or herself, and is an integral part of the totality of who they are. Without the other person each of them is incomplete in the relationship that they have chosen.

We must recognize that in many situations women have not felt that this is true. Rather we have sensed that we must sacrifice ourselves completely, or we must stop being ourselves and become what our husband is, or we must please him even though we never consider what might please us. Should we do so, we would feel guilty because we know that our role is to serve and help others, not them helping or serving us. Again, this is not biblical! Both the man and the woman need to make personal sacrifices, they must give of themselves to the relationship, they must learn to express their desires and their strongest needs, and each must learn to give in to the other so as to build a special relationship for their marriage. Becoming "one flesh" is a mutual task for all of life.

Without a doubt the statement, "Therefore a man leaves his father and his mother and clings to his wife, and they become one flesh" (Genesis 2:24), emphasizes this aspect of the unity and the companionship of the couple and the strong attraction of their love. For both man and woman the companionship and their new unity is even more important than the family ties that were so emphasized in Hebrew society. This same process continues to be an essential step toward truly becoming "one flesh", which should be the goal of a Christian marriage.

"Submit yourselves to one another out of reverence for Christ" - Ephesians 5:21

The Bible brings God's message to help us understand how we are to live and relate to Him and to others. However, we need to remember that the Bible is also the product of a specific time and culture. It is imperative that we understand the historical and cultural setting, the "then and there" of Scripture, so that we can best understand God's word for the "here and now." When we read the Bible legalistically, without taking the historical and cultural setting into consideration and without recognition of the freedom for which Christ has freed us, we enslave ourselves anew, imposing restrictions on ourselves and others that God has not intended. (See again John 8:31-32 and 36.)

Paul confronted very specific moral and relational problems in the young churches of the first century. We can see this especially in the letters to the Corinthians where he gives instructions that speak specifically to the Christians of that city where there were so many moral issues. When these passages are taken out of context and interpreted in a legalistic way the body of Christ suffers, and surely Christ must suffer as He sees the broken lives that result from these restrictive interpretations and applications that spoke to specific situations "then and there" being imposed in the "here and now."

When we find ourselves faced with interpretations of this nature, we should look at Paul's Magna Carta in Galatians 3:28 to see his culminating idea of what the faith community should be. "There is no longer Jew or Greek, there is no longer slave or free, there is no longer male and female; for all of you are one in Christ Jesus."

I have chosen the letter to the Ephesians for the third emphasis that I want to give on marriage. "Be subject to one another out of reverence to Christ" (Ephesians 5:21).

This passage in Ephesians 5:21-6:9, together with Colossians 3:18-4:1 and 1 Peter 3:1-7 contain the "Domestic Codes," norms and regulations for the Christian family. These were adapted from those of the society in which they lived, and reflect the extreme rabbinical position of the day in which the customs and prejudices of the society that had enslaved women are maintained. In the use of these "Domestic Codes" as we find in the Bible, one sees the tremendous effort of the leaders of the church to avoid any conduct among Christians that would cause problems with the communities in which they lived. They feared that any deviation of Christian women from the norm of society would bring persecution on the young church struggling to grow and to survive in an already hostile environment. The specter of a persecution that might bring an end to the early Christian movement was a constant concern for its leaders. For this reason, the Domestic Codes are seen as a reflection of the society and culture in which they lived; the proper, traditional roles of society that must be maintained at whatever cost. Women must be "kept in their place," and so the use of the term "submit" or "be subject" is used. However, in this case, it is preceded by the statement, "Be subject to one another out of reverence for Christ." In the Christian family all were to be subject one to another. This was the difference that Christ had made! There was not to be a hierarchy or a certain few who were to be subject to another person, but all, one to another.

I want to emphasize that we do not find a single rule or norm that speaks of domestic submission such as found in the Domestic Codes from the lips of Christ. Nor do we find it in the way that He lived and carried out His ministry, nor is it found in the growth and practice of the early church as found in the book of Acts. Even Paul's letters show how he sends greetings to his co-laborers, both women and men. As a result, for me, to take these passages in which we find the Domestic Codes as normative for the Christian woman is a mistake that leads to enslavement, and frequently mistreatment and abuse, and is against the teaching of Christ who has made us free, both women and men. Christ in no way gave this type of hierarchy to get closer to God. He offered Himself to all, men and women, as the way to the Father. The example of Christ, in word and deed, is that of a servant offering to all the way of life, life both abundant and eternal.

Read carefully Ephesians chapters 4, 5, and 6, where Paul emphasizes the basic idea of the new life in Christ. Each section in these three chapters begins with a basic teaching followed by an explication of how this specific teaching can be developed in the life of the believer. We have already mentioned this in Chapter 3, but it is important to reiterate this here because of the context given by Paul to the Domestic Code and the way in which he subtly changes the way in which it will be carried out, beginning with verse 21. There is to be mutual submission.

How many times have we heard a sermon or a teaching of how women should submit themselves to their husbands, and that the husband should love his wife. But how many times have you heard this key verse (v. 21) presented as the key to a good marriage and the marriage relationship? I believe that this is the most correct and perceptive teaching on marriage that we find in the teachings of Paul. Mutual submission, a self-accepted willingness to limit oneself because of the love and respect that each feels for the other, in reverence for Christ our Lord is a firm and solid base for marriage and one that should be practiced by all Christians.

We should recognize that Paul lived in a world that was restrictive and limiting for him as Christ's apostle and missionary. Both those inside and outside of the church frequently criticized him. One of the biggest problems of the early church was their misuse of the freedom that Christ had given them. There were excesses in their worship services and in the Lord's Supper; freedom meant libertine behavior for some church members. As a result, little by little Paul and other leaders began to make more and more restrictions on the churches as well as individual Christians. There were more and more rules and regulations for order and control in every sphere of life. The great growth of the church and the freedom they had enjoyed during the years following the death, resurrection and ascension of Christ came to an end, bringing a strict, legalistic, limiting expression of the church in its polity and practice, one that deviated radically from the teachings and practice of Christ. All have suffered from such an imposition, but especially women. Even today, you and I suffer its consequences, as do women all over the Christian world.

"Submit to one another out of reverence for Christ" can never be a legally imposed norm. It must be something that one chooses voluntarily as a follower of Christ who wants to walk in His footsteps. I firmly believe that seeking a goal for our mutual good such as this; being willing to accept personal limitations for our mutual development; showing love and respect one to the other that promotes a sense of "belonging" and partnership; will produce a firm and lasting relationship, one that will bring happiness and growth to each spouse, as well as to the couple itself.

In this section (Ephesians 5:21-33) Paul is speaking of the duties of both husband and wife in the marital relationship. And as he begins we see the analogy of marriage to the relation of Christ to His church. In different passages Paul uses three metaphors for the church: the body with Christ as the head (Colossians 1:24); the temple or the household with Christ as the cornerstone (Ephesians 2:19); and marriage, with Christ as the husband, the passage that is being considered here.

The wife is to relate to her husband in submission as she submits to the Lord. But immediately Paul says that the husband is to love his wife, just as Christ loved His church and gave His life for it (V. 25). The concept of love was not one that was emphasized in the marital relationship at this time. This was a revolutionary idea! A man was to *love* his wife! Paul goes on to explain more in detail. This love of the husband for his wife should be the same as the love he has for himself and his body. It should be manifested in nurture and tender care of the wife, just as Christ cares for the church. Paul reiterates that he is speaking here of the church, but he adds, "Each of you, however, should love his wife as himself, and a wife should respect her husband" (Ephesians 5:33). Again, the idea of mutual submission and mutual love is the key to a loving and sustainable marriage.

I believe that the three biblical concepts that have been presented in this chapter are basic to understanding woman's role as a wife: the "help-meet," becoming "one flesh;" and "submit yourselves one to the other, in reverence for Christ." We have affirmed that both men, as well as women, will benefit from such a relationship. Remember that each partner is distinct one from the other and thus each will bring her/his own perspective to the marriage, different desires, different abilities, different ways of doing things, but it is truly a wonderful gift (grace) of God that each can work, both separately and together, for the development of the marriage relationship.

Marriage is an institution established by God that offers men and women, created in His image, the opportunity to end their loneliness and separateness and have a life of union, companionship and blessed significance. It is a life that permits maximum development of our individuality, of who we are as men and women, gifted with spiritual gifts, capabilities and responsibilities. However, at the same time, recognizing our need for unity and companionship, we are able to develop ways that strengthen the relationship and make it a stabilizing force for society and for the family and an increasingly meaningful and lasting experience for the couple.

Activities for reflection and learning

1. Write a "I remember…" outline/diary of the period of your engagement, noting the most important events that brought you to your marriage. How do you feel as you remember these events? Do they bring you happiness and enthusiasm for your marriage? If not, why not? Are these issues that you and your husband can address?

2. One of the tasks that every adult needs to do is to express gratitude for their life and for events that have made it significant: to God, to parents, to your husband, and to other special people. Reflect on your life and the things for which you should express thanks. Make a list of these people and the things for which you should thank them. Keep the list nearby so that you can add other things that come to your mind for which you need to express your gratitude. Seek opportunities daily to express your gratitude to these people, but especially your husband.

   What do you think about making the effort to become more of a grateful person?

   It's a good thing to do; it can change your life — and your marriage!

3. Select four of the Beatitudes (Matthew 5:3-12) and meditate on the characteristics presented in each. The word "blessed" means "happiness," or "happy." Write a paragraph about how practicing each of these characteristics could make your marriage happier. Are there decisions that you need to make as a result of this study and reflection?

4. Share with your husband the result of your reflection about marriage after reading this chapter and doing these activities: about your role as a wife, and what you think about your life as a couple. Listen attentively to his response and together make decisions how to improve your marriage.

Questions to answer alone or in a group

- Note five ways in which you can be a "help-meet" to your husband, and five ways that you feel that he can be a "help-meet" for you. Is the second list as valid as the first? Why or why not?

- What are the essential characteristics for becoming "one flesh?"

- What is the thing that most bothers you most about submitting to another person?

  What is the thing that you like the most about submitting to another person? Give reasons for your answers.

6. When the Relationship Is Shaken

> You, therefore, beloved, since you are forewarned, beware
> that you are not carried away with the error of the
> lawless and lose your own stability. But grow in the grace
> and knowledge of our Lord and Savior Jesus Christ. To
> Him be the glory both now and to the day of eternity.
> Amen. 2 Peter 3:17, 18

Many women are very romantic and idealistic in their ideas about marriage: "they married and lived happily ever after." It sounds so beautiful, so perfect, precisely what a woman, faithful to her psychological and spiritual formation, desires for her life.

So when the first conflicts and the difficult relationships in the marriage arrive, she doesn't know what to do. She blames herself; she hides it from her family, from her spouse, and, in many ways, from herself. As a result the tensions grow and the relationship is shaken.

In today's world there are other women, perhaps more "sophisticated" from a worldly point of view who approach the marital relationship with the attitude of "if it doesn't work out, we can separate or divorce. There is no need to live a life of martyrdom such as I have seen my mother or other women live."

Neither the first way of facing this problem nor the second are healthy approaches in marriage. Neither can bring about happiness and the growth of each spouse nor develop the relationship itself. In this chapter we will search for healthier ways to respond to problems in the marital relationship, when the marriage is "on shaky ground." But first of all, let's consider some of the causes and their manifestations that are found in a marriage that is facing problems.

Difficulties in the relationship

It is not easy to live with someone, to try to become "one flesh," to form an intimate relationship among spouses. Before you know it there are frictions and small irritations that may be the first symptoms of more profound problems. Whatever they may be, if they are not attended to they will grow and cause division, bitterness, resentments, and finally the break-up of the marriage.

Marriage is the *union* of two persons, but problems and difficulties can cause *dis-union* or separation. Instead of being a "help-meet" to the other, each becomes a hindrance to the other and causes major problems for the marriage. Instead of being "one flesh," each spouse emphasizes and develops his/her own way. Instead of submitting to each other out of reverence for Christ, each looks out for his/her own interests and follows his/her own uncontrolled egotism.

Perhaps the most frequently mentioned difficulty in marriage that causes it to be shaken to its roots is the incompatibility of characters. Incompatibility is the inability to be together in harmony; it is when two people are opposites in character, and discordant in their interests and actions. There is no doubt that this situation exists in many marriages. The two spouses thought during their engagement that they had found the ideal person, but now he/she "does not understand me." Or, they had thought, "I don't like this little thing he/she does, but they'll change once we're married," and no change has been achieved. There are both conscious and unconscious causes for the reality of these complaints. It is difficult to become "one flesh", to make necessary changes that can promote harmony and happiness. You do well to make every effort to resolve these difficulties together and perhaps with the help of an understanding, empathic pastor or counselor.

Sarcasm causes your partner to have a twisted view of the marriage

One of the causes of this *dis-union* is egotism. A happy and stable marriage requires that both persons work daily to eliminate their egotistical tendencies, of considering themselves only, of not taking into account the needs and interests of the other person, but rather just of themselves. This is very different from a healthy attitude of individuality, as we have previously explained. Egotism is seen when the person only thinks of him/herself, considering others only as instruments for his/her own gratification. This person sees other people without value or importance in comparison to his own personal and unchecked interests and desires.

There are spouses who try to destroy the healthy self-concept that their partner has of her/himself. They use sarcasm frequently, causing the person to doubt his/her value and to have a twisted or distorted view of his/her personal life, as well as their value to the marriage. This form of cruelty results in the person doubting him/herself and being confused as to his/her role as a person as well as a spouse.

Another cause of *dis-union* is to take the other person for granted. It is the habit of thinking that they will always be there, that they can be counted on at any time, no matter what happens. This is precisely the antithesis of mutual trust and belonging of which we have spoken in the previous chapter. To take a person for granted, and to treat him/her as just an object in their world, to which one has become accustomed, is very dehumanizing. Not only is the person not taken into consideration, it is as if the other person is so accustomed to having him/her there that they don't even consider the importance of their attitudes, their thoughts, their wishes, or their possibilities. It is as if they assume the position of the other, they can "speak for" or "act for" them without consultation. Such an attitude robs the person of his/her value as an individual and gives them a de-personalized value, such as that of a piece of furniture or some other thing, perhaps preferred but many times forgotten.

Another cause of *dis-union* is silence. This is the silence that penetrates and destroys the totality of the relationship. Constant silence between spouses is the sign that something has gone wrong. Communication is basic to the relationship; constant silence shows that there is no longer such a relationship. Silence can be manifested in many ways: lack of words; lack of activities; lack of participation in the common life of the couple. They may talk, but not of private thoughts, but of those which are peripheral to the relationship. They no longer participate together in significant activities, but in those which are lacking in significance.

Another problem is in the area of sexual difficulties. The lack of mutual understanding can cause problems in their sex life and *dis-union* in their relationship. In our day and time when there is so much emphasis and publicity oriented to sexuality, it is very easy to be influenced by this focus which many times is not only wrong, but also prompted by the media, and totally hedonistic.

Sexual relations should be a symbol of the union of the couple, not just a physical expression of the love that each has for the other. A healthy open attitude to the sexual aspect of marriage on the part of each spouse is of supreme importance. As a result there will be a greater possibility of satisfaction between the two and for each one. It is very worthwhile to make an honest and sensible effort to express your feelings about your relationship with your husband to him, and that he do the same with you.

A serious problem that many married couples face is the interference in their marriage by other people. These may be family members, many times the mother of one or the other, or possibly of both, but it can also be their longtime friends. Marriage does not do away with these relationships, but these should occupy a different position from that which they had previously. Now the primary relationship is the marriage and these other relationships must not be allowed to cause conflict between the couple. Should such conflicts occur careful attention should be given to reaching an understanding of the situation and agreeing on limitations and ways of confronting the issue when necessary.

The "other person" can be a friend of the opposite sex, male or female. This can become a threat for the marriage. It can be someone at work, in the university, in sports activities, in the church, but little by little the friendship becomes more significant to the person. While these begin as sincere friendships, often they can lead to infidelity. Infidelity is not only the sexual act with someone who is not your spouse, but it can be in other areas of relationship – constant presence, taking excess time with the person instead of with the spouse, thinking about the person, among many others. A married man or woman should avoid allowing him/herself to develop such relationships. If there is any indication of being with or thinking about the other person constantly, it should be terminated at once. Loyalty and fidelity in marriage is essential to its durability and its happiness.

This problem is even more complicated in our day and time. In our contemporary life, in television and in the movies, infidelity is taken as natural and commonplace. There is permissiveness and a sense of inevitability that it will occur in all marriages. It is presented as something so attractive and essential for one's happiness and development that there should be no problem with it. This spirit pervades the world in which the marriage is lived out and creates many problems for married couples. For their marriage to survive, a couple must work hard to maintain their loyalty to each other in thought, in attitude and in action.

Economic difficulties can be a major factor in marital problems. It requires special effort on the part of each spouse and all the members of the family to be able to resolve their corrosive action in the relationship. Especially in times of economic down turn and financial problems on every front, the couple needs to work together on the family and personal budgets, finding ways to economize and live within the budget.

In many families in today's world it is necessary that both spouses work outside the home, but they need to decide together, as a couple, how they will use the money earned by each of them. Their income should be considered as a common source earned by the two of them in order to maintain a functional family budget. If there is only one salary coming into the family, it should be considered as money earned by the family. Many times the wife and homemaker is relegated to be a person without a sense of identity because she doesn't earn a salary. For many women the only way open to them to have a bit of money for their own needs or expenses is to take it from the household expenses. This is a very sad situation for all the family because it places the woman (wife and mother) in a very inferior position and at the same time promotes manipulation, deception, and other inappropriate forms of survival. No woman should have to resort to such measures.

Perhaps the greatest and most difficult problems to solve are the attitudes both conscious and unconscious that have to do with roles, relationships, values and experiences. Everyone comes to marriage with certain preconceived ideas and with a scale of values already well defined. Many times these are very different between the two spouses. They should have talked about these things before entering in the marriage, but frequently these are not mentioned in an open way during the engagement period. These differences can cause great *dis-union* in the marriage, causing lack of trust, bitterness, insecurity, and other negative attitudes. As time progresses these attitudes can lead to aggression and violence, or one or both of the spouses will disengage emotionally and/or physically from the relationship.

There are special problems for women who are full-time "stay-at-home Moms" and also for those who work outside the home, but also are responsible for caring for the home in their "second job." In both cases the woman needs the support, encouragement and help of her spouse. In many occasions the "stay at home Mom," who also is working all day long, is bored from only talking with the children and caring for their needs and those of her family all day, every day. She longs for adult conversation, and for adult companionship. For the woman who works outside the home, she begins her "second job" when she arrives at home following a full day of work already. Many times she will have picked up her children from the day care on the way home. She is tired and tense, and there is much to do. When her efforts are neither appreciated by her family nor is help offered by her spouse, her situation can become extremely stressful and depressing. In each of these cases a very dangerous situation for the marriage can develop and little by little the relationship will be shaken and can eventually fall. The husband in each of these cases, the "stay at home mom" or the wife who works outside the home, needs to help his wife in the work that needs to be done in the home. They need to have a division of responsibilities and work together in maintaining the family and the home. In addition, planning to have some time together as a couple outside the home can be a "lifesaver" for the beleaguered wife. As the children grow and are able they should be given tasks to help in the home according to their age level and abilities. Every member of the family can and should help maintain the family home and share in the tasks that need to be done.

Another cause for the *dis-union* between spouses is the desire to be happy. How many times do we hear someone say, "He/she doesn't make me happy." Truthfully, this is impossible because no one can make another happy. They can promote the happiness of the other, they can create a climate in which happiness can emerge and develop, but only the person him/herself can make themselves happy. It is the person that makes the decision for happiness, of how he/she will react in a given situation. Happiness is a great gift, but it does not depend alone on the relationship with the other person or what they do to bring happiness to a situation. The attitude we have toward life can bring happiness even in the midst of problems. (See Habakkuk 3:17-19 as an example.) The choice is ours to a great extent. Interestingly, in the book of Proverbs, one proverb is found twice that speaks about the power to destroy happiness by being contentious or quarrelsome. "It is better to live in a corner of the rooftop than in a house shared with a contentious wife" (Proverbs 21:9 and 25:24) and again, "It is better to live in a desert land than with a contentious and fretful wife" (Proverbs 21:19). Certainly, this truth is applicable to men as well, but it reminds us very graphically how important it is to find healthy ways of solving problems within marriage.

Many other difficulties present themselves in the marital relationship; some are variations of those we have mentioned, and others are different. Whatever they may be, they should be considered as problems for the marriage and the husband and wife should work together to find ways of resolving them. A happy marriage is not a marriage without problems, but one in which problems are faced with vision and hope, and with a firm dedication and commitment to the relationship and to their spouse.

Painful confrontations

All the difficulties that we have mentioned to this point are causes of pain and distress in marriage, but separation causes a very special pain and hurt, one that requires the special attention of each spouse, of their family, their friends and others of significance to the couple. Many times the factors that have produced the separation have been small at first, things that seemed insignificant, but that grew and grew and became so large that they brought about a real break in the relationship and separation became a reality.

Separation can be temporary, or it can become final or lead to divorce, but whatever the case, it is always sad and painful, because marriage is meant for *union*, not *dis-union*. Nevertheless, one must recognize that there are some marriages that simply do not work and never will work. In other words, there are marriages that are not *unions*, but relationships in which there are so many differences that the couple has no capacity or desire to work toward forming a *union*. They do not see that they have any compatibility for a lifelong commitment. Even though one of the partners may want to "keep trying", in many situations this only prolongs the toxic relationship and in the long run does even more harm to the couple and to their family. Facing these conditions, separation or divorce should not be seen as a defeat, but rather as a challenge for each person to recognize the causes which have led to this *dis-union,* as well as the necessity of making decisions for personal change to rebuild their life following the separation.

When confrontations begin to build up in number and intensity in a marriage, they tend to produce some immediate form of separation. There are many causes for these painful confrontations, many of which we have already mentioned. However there are some confrontations that worsen the relationship more quickly than others.

The first is the lack of commitment to the marriage. This is a problem that has grown in our day and time. I do not believe that in years past people entered marriage thinking, "if it doesn't work, I can get a divorce or make another arrangement." However, it is very common to find this thought in today's world. Previously many marriages did not work, and many couples lived apart, but divorce was not a viable solution. Many times, in these cases, the husband lived with another woman and had children with her, but usually the original wife was left alone with the children of the marriage. There is no doubt that these situations caused a great deal of pain for the family and for each family member.

Unfortunately today there is much less commitment to marriage as an institution. In order for a marriage to survive and be meaningful for each spouse, there must be a high degree of commitment to the relationship and a willingness to make every effort to preserve it and make it more meaningful for each spouse.

There will always be stresses and tensions in marriage, and the partners must make a special effort so that the marriage can face these tensions and overcome them. Our commitment and firm belief in the relationship is an indispensable factor to be able to face these tensions adequately.

Another attitude that causes many problems for marriage is the belief that marriage exists just for procreation, to give birth to children and to provide them with a home. Many families who believe this go from one extreme to another, from a time of feuding to a time of truce, and back again. Truthfully, they live in "a cold war", which leaves every member insecure, unhappy and in limbo.

Children are important to the marriage, and it is important to provide a united and nurturing home for them, but the true foundation of marriage is the couple. They form the principle base of the family. It is their relationship that should be maintained and developed. When this relationship is good, the sincere desire to have a good and healthy family for their children springs forth spontaneously. When the couple feels that their children are a weight on their hands, or that their responsibility is just to tolerate or put up with their children, then the marriage and the family are going to suffer greatly.

There is a very sad situation that exists in some marriages among fellow believers. When their marriage begins to have problems and is on "shaky ground", they think, "Everything will work out since we are Christians." As a result they do not make the effort to resolve the problems that separate them, because they believe that it will work itself out because of their relationship with God. Many times one of the spouses, or possibly both of them, blames the other for their lack of faith or for their sin, or for their inability to follow the plan of God. Others place a tremendous load of guilt on themselves assuming that they are the cause of the problem. Each of these situations takes away the joy of their salvation and they are left without this wonderful resource for maintaining happiness and joy in their lives. Sooner or later the marriage will fail and the painful wounds and the lingering perplexity will remain with them for the rest of their life.

Nowhere in the Bible does God promise us that all our relationships are going to work out well, nor that we do not need to make the effort to solve the problems in our marriage. However, it is wonderful to know that as believers we have the power and the direction of God in our marriage and family. He helps us in all the situations in which we find ourselves, but we are responsible to recognize the problem and its causes, to seek the precise help needed, and to work with the Lord in finding the correct solutions.

Jesus directs us as to the attitude that we should have in our marriage when He taught about the commandment, "Do not kill." (See Matthew 5:21-26.) He does not excuse the person who says, "I am innocent. I have never killed anyone." Rather He goes to the heart of the problem, and speaks of rage and of words that come out of our mouths when we are angry, words that destroy the personality of the other person (and, truly, as perpetrators of this rage, our own personality, also), and cause the loss of hope, both personally and for the marriage. When we find ourselves in situations such as these we must take an active role in solving this destructive pattern.

Jesus gives such importance to our problem of anger and how it can destroy relationships that He says that if you know that someone has something against you, you should interrupt the most sacred moment of worship, leaving your offering at the altar and go and find the person you have offended in order to be reconciled with him/her. Following the reconciliation, then you can return and present your offering to God. If this is the way of reconciliation indicated by Jesus for social relations, how much

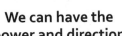

We can have the power and direction of God in our marriage.

more should it be the way for a married couple! Anger hurts and destroys relationships; reconciliation offers the possibility of forgiveness and re-commitment to the marriage. (Read Matthew 5:21-26.)

Another situation that produces serious problems in marriage is the result of accumulated tensions and the lack of adequate ways of facing and solving them. Tolerance of repeated frustrations will reach its climax and the person will explode saying things that wound their spouse, and many times insulting him/her. The cause of coming to this level of tension is that the person does not know how to talk about the differences he/she has with the other person, and so he/she puts up with it until finally there is an explosion. Sometimes the reason for the tension building up to explosion level is that the person thinks a

Christian should not get angry and so they keep suppressing their anger. They do so until they can't continue any longer, and in this moment of extreme tension words are said that aggravate the situation, bringing on physical and emotional separation or d*is-union.*

Divorce is more and more common in our days, both among Christians and those who are not Christians. In spite of the fact that it is more common, we should never forget that when the relationship is destroyed, not only the couple, but the whole family suffers. As Christian women who want to maintain and improve relationships in their family, we must seek ways of solution to our marital problems and, along with our husband, determine to grow together in our marriage. The task before us is daunting, but the presence and help of Christ are our sure means of hope. Now let's consider some other helps available to us when our marriage is on "shaky ground."

Possible solutions

Women, as we have seen previously, are oriented psychologically and spiritually toward relationships. When these relationships are destroyed, or when their foundation is shaken, women suffer tremendously. So every effort must be made to build firm foundations and avoid the possibility that these relations should end in defeat and permanent *dis-union.*

Without a doubt, the most important thing to do so that the relationship will endure and be meaningful for the couple, is for each of them to prepare adequately for marriage.

What should this preparation include? I think that it should begin in childhood, giving emphasis to the holistic and integral preparation of the individual: their values, their attitudes, their ability to be understanding, tolerant, positive, realistic and hopeful in their relationships with other people. During their growth from childhood to young adulthood, each individual should develop specific criteria that they consider necessary for marriage, their own role and that of the spouse. These criteria should be used in the selection of the person with whom they will share their life in marriage. They must be sure that these same criteria are valued and shared by the person who will become their spouse and that together they can strive toward these high ideals. These criteria should be the constant point of reference for their marriage, giving stability when problems arise, and giving them a vision and commitment beyond the problem/s at hand.

Another important element that must be emphasized in marriage is *understanding*. This should be seen in each spouse. In his excellent book, *To Understand Each Other,* Swiss psychiatrist Paul Tournier[14] emphasizes that the couple must work together to understand each another: they must desire to understand one another and constantly work toward this goal. Nevertheless, instead of allowing each one to be who he/she is and working toward understanding her/him, we hear the sad words, "I cannot understand him/her." These words indicate that the person is not willing to recognize that their spouse is different from him/her, that he/she thinks and acts in very distinct ways. In order to understand one another it is necessary to work at it constantly, to love each other, and together bring their lives under the control and direction of the Lord Jesus. Understanding one another is based on unconditional acceptance one of the other and the disposition and the desire of achieving the goal of empathic understanding for each other.

Another possible solution is to be willing to identify correctly the causes of conflict. This can be very painful, but it is essential in order to resolve the reasons for conflict in our marriage. Many times we identify one thing as the cause of our problem, when in reality it is only the symptom of the real problem. The identification must treat not only the causes of conflict, but also the sentiments of each person relative to the problem. It may be that for one person it is a problem of large proportion, while for the other, it has only relatively minor implications. While each must learn to respect and honor the perspective of the other, the correct identification of the causes of conflict is indispensable in order to resolve it.

Sometimes a spouse will think that their ideas or feelings are insignificant, or when faced with the complexity of a problem, they don't want to cause more problems or "rock the boat," and so they remain silent. Or perhaps they have such a poor self-esteem and think that the other person is "so good," and that they are "so bad," that they should not speak up and share their feelings. You must avoid this sort of self-evaluation in situations where it is essential that the perspective of both spouses is taken into consideration. In spite of the fact that you have not shared your real feelings and ideas previously, you must be honest with yourself and with your spouse. The admonition of Paul in Ephesians should guide us in these circumstances,

> "But, speaking the truth in love, we must grow up
> in every way into Him who is the head, into Christ, from
> whom the whole body, joined and knit together by every

ligament with which it is equipped, as each part is working properly, promotes the body's growth in building itself up in love." (Ephesians 4:15-16)

Confrontation based in mutual honesty and love will produce growth and improvement in the marital relationship, and will be an important step toward possible solutions of problems.

The tension faced in daily life as well as that in the marital relationship itself combine to produce stress in the marriage, and in each spouse. This can gravely complicate the relationship. It is necessary to learn ways to reduce the tension, including relaxation techniques, tension reduction exercises, and ways of redirecting the tension into more positive avenues of behavior.

Giving full course to the tension causes pain and wounds that perhaps will never heal. When you notice that the tension in the home is growing, you should find some way to reduce the tension in that moment. For example, if you have been working very hard on some project, change and do something else for a while. It is necessary to break the pattern of doing just one thing on and on. Go for a walk, go shopping, exercise, or do some other activity. If you have been working on something that demanded your full attention for some time, try to do something light hearted or humorous. This change of pace can be a wonderful aid to relaxation. The emotional equilibrium found in practicing the extremes on the continuum between solitary/gregarious, serious/spontaneous, positive/negative, dependable/reckless, independent/dependent will help to reduce the level of tension in the marriage. Try it, and you will see the benefit of practicing these extremes. Truthfully we all have these dichotomies in our personality even though we find one or another to be more "who we are." But opening yourself to the total spectrum of your personality will be helpful to reducing the tension you experience in your marriage. In appreciating the differences in our own personality it will allow you to appreciate those in your spouses also.

The biblical teaching about "taking off" and "putting on" is very applicable to marriage. One must eliminate certain characteristics, attitudes and actions that are negative and destructive and replace them with others that are positive and that promote enhancing and building up the relationship. Every spouse will know of certain things that need to be changed, but if you find it hard to articulate them, look up the list in Colossians 3:5-17 to help you become more sensitive to things that need to be changed in your marriage, things you need to "take off" and others to "put on."

A great help to resolve these problems is to keep your marriage and your relationship with your husband up to date. Avoid letting difficulties or tensions build up and go on from day to day. It is much better, and easier, to solve them when they are small, and not waiting, thinking they will disappear, when in reality they will grow even larger, or worse still, they will be denied and take an even greater emotional toll on the marriage and on each person. One counselor has suggested that each week the couple should have a specific time to talk and "get things off their chest." Thus they can take care of smaller irritations and other difficulties or misunderstandings that have come up before they get out of hand.

The solution that is sought in these conflict situations should be one of a workable integration of the two positions. When the only desire is to "have your own way," the major outcome will be more polarization on the part of each person, causing even more difficulties for the marriage. The idea that for one to win, the other has to lose is fatal for the marital relation. David Augsburger,[15] pastoral counselor, professor and author of *Personal Problems? Treat Them with Love,* emphasizes this aspect of interpersonal conflict. The sense of mutuality in the relationship must take precedence over the idea of "having my own way," and that of "I win, you lose." Without a doubt this is only possible when love reigns in the relationship and gives strength to the couple to work toward finding ways to strengthen the relationship. This is a good attitude that should become a constant challenge for the couple.

In marriage each person is responsible for his/her ideas, thoughts, attitudes, and must also be responsible for searching for ways in which difficulties can be resolved.

Open and honest communication is essential to resolve the tensions and for building up the relationship. There are persons who pride themselves on their honesty, but who use their honesty to control and intimidate others, not to better the relationship. Honesty should be motivated by love and mutual consideration and in this form the two spouses can grow in love and mutual appreciation. Remember that we have noted previously that when someone loves another they seek their happiness and their growth. Contrary to what some believe, it is necessary to confront marriage difficulties with love so that the relationship will continue to grow adequately.

If you want to have more peace and understanding in the family and in your marital relationships you should begin by thanking God for the person that He has given you and for what this person signifies for you. Thinking about your spouse, reflect on the following:

1. The happiest experience that you have had with him/her.

2. The time when you felt closest to your spouse.

3. Ways in which your life has become better because of him/her.

4. Things that you have learned from your spouse that have made your life better.

After reflecting on these experiences, and giving thanks to God for what your spouse means to you, go to him/her and tell him/her the reasons why you are grateful for them. Be specific. Tell the person exactly how you feel about these more significant moments in your relationship. Be precise when you explain what you have learned from him/her and describe the most significant things that he/she has done for you. Rejoice together in these moments of honesty and love.

Another great help for strengthening the marital relationship is to know how to forgive one another. There are both small and large things that can happen between spouses. It is very sad when instead of pardoning and forgetting, a list of grievances is kept, and in the least expected moment brought out to accuse and attack the other person. To forgive one another we must be sincere in doing so. We must learn to forgive according to the biblical example: forgiveness that erases the memory, one that promotes relationship and helps it become more meaningful each day.

The following words of Paul Tournier are a call to Christian men and women to understand the importance of our faith in bringing about a deeper understanding of God's purpose for marriage and thus one of the most important possible solutions to misunderstandings within marriage:

> "There is a need for bringing faith and life together, if
> faith is to make a difference and if life is to be transformed.
> A bringing together of faith and marital life is needed, so that
> faith may bring its incomparable transforming power and
> its understanding, and so that marital life may attain its
> fullness.
> "How can the two be brought together? That depends
> less upon what we do than upon what we are. It is more a
> matter of attitude than of method. We can at any rate ask
> God to lead us there, to show us the way, Himself to bring

about this total unity which is, according to His plan, to be the experience of marriage."[16]

The marital relationship may become shaky even in the most stable marriage. So it's worthwhile to reflect on these possible solutions for resolving conflict. Don't criticize yourself or your spouse unmercifully because of the difficulties you are experiencing, rather look for the causes of the problems and ways in which they can be resolved. God will bless you in this sincere effort to improve your marriage and make the relationship healthier and more significant for each of you and for your family.

Activities for reflection and learning

1. Write down three problems you have had in your marriage, indicating the cause and/or events that precipitated the problem. Note how you managed the problem, how you feel about it now, and, in retrospect, what would you have done differently for a better outcome. What can you learn from this experience?

2. Write a paragraph on your belief about marriage. Try to reflect realistically about the relationship, giving several days to this consideration as you search for your most perceptive beliefs. This is an activity that would be very beneficial to do with your husband. Talk together about your beliefs and determine if they are reflected in your marriage or not. After this reflection together, write a "Marriage Creed" or "What I Believe about Marriage" that expresses your beliefs.

3. Study Matthew 7:24-27, reflecting on the foundation of marriage and the conditions that can cause difficulties for the relationship. Mention some of the problems you have experienced and how they affected your marriage. What do Jesus' words signify for you and your marriage, "Everyone who listens to these words of Mine and acts on them will be like a wise man who built his house on rock"?

4. What counsel can you give to a person whose marriage is on "shaky ground?" Will the ideas considered in this chapter help you to give a more perceptive answer?

Questions to answer alone or in a group

- Define marriage, separation, and divorce. What is the basic relationship of God with the person/s in each case?

- Make a list of problems that can happen in marriage, including attitudes and actions. Then grade each one as to how it affects the relationship, beginning with the greatest problem and going to the smallest. What can you do to eliminate the possibility of these problems putting your marriage "on shaky ground?" Consider each one separately.

- What can you do daily to maintain the health and significance of your marriage?

  What can you do when your marriage begins to "shake" or be "on shaky ground"?

7. As a Mother

> *I am grateful to God – whom I worship with a clear*
> *conscience, as my ancestors did – when I remember you*
> *constantly in my prayers night and day....I am reminded*
> *of your sincere faith, a faith that lived first in your*
> *grandmother Lois and your mother Eunice and now,*
> *I am sure, lives in you.* 2 Timothy 1:3, 5

God has always planned that each individual would have their family as the center of their formation and the setting for their life. Psalm 68:5 and 6 help us understand the importance God gave to the family relationship. "A father to the fatherless, a defender of widows, is God in His holy dwelling. God sets the lonely in families...." (NIV). The calling of Abraham emphasizes the significance of the person and the family: "In you all the families of the earth shall be blessed" or the alternate reading, "by you all the families of the earth shall bless themselves" (Genesis 12:3.) The blessing of being a part of a good family is to be cherished and passed on in blessing from generation to generation.

Another evidence of the importance that God gives to the family is that He chose a family to be the earthly nurturing setting for His only Son. The Bible tells us that in this family, "Jesus grew in wisdom and in stature, and in favor with God and with men" (Luke 2:52.) God founded the family, recognizing that loneliness and isolation were not what His creation needed. There was a need for communication, for relationship and belonging. So, to reach this end, the family became the basic institution in society.

Today the family has many problems. Brusque and rapid societal changes have left social institutions shaken. What yesterday was sure and valued today cannot be depended on and is of little or no value for many. There are new values, many times very strange to those who have not experienced them before. In a world that continues to become more global and pluralistic, values that were once sacrosanct are now considered to be "out of touch" with the demands of modern life. The Christian family finds itself attacked from every side by new models of what it is to be a family as well as demands placed upon it to remain faithful to its roots. So, let's look at the family to see what the role of women and mothers is today.

What is a family?

Someone has said that a family is a "small social system in which individuals are related through reciprocal affection and loyalty, and in which a relationship is formed that lasts for years or decades. Its members enter by birth, adoption or marriage, and leave only through death." This definition is a good starting place. We can add to this definition that the family, in all its variations, is the product of the creative purpose of God, and exists in response to the need of humanity to live in community. Although in every family there is the seed of God's plan, however distorted it may have become, the communal relationship is viable only when the family acknowledges and expresses the creative purpose of God.

1. Basic concepts of the family

It is more and more difficult to define the family because in our post-modern world there are many different "varieties" of families. Nevertheless we are going to give some concepts that can help us to have a functional definition for our study and reflection.

1. The family is a permanent social system. Even when the person is distanced from the family, it does not mean that the relationship is terminated or the "presence" of the person does not exist. Often the "presence" of the estranged or missing family member is even stronger than when he/she was actually present.

2. The family maintains this relationship through ties of affection more than through ties of productivity or the execution of a specific job. Mutual love is essential for the formation of each person.

3. Every member of the family has special needs to be satisfied. The family as the basic societal institution should supply to a large extent the following needs of its members:

- Security or survival needs. These needs must be met before the person can give him/herself to other developmental needs.

- Human development needs: intellectual, emotional, physical and spiritual.

- Personal psycho-social needs, such as

  - to be valued as a person,
  - to be loved and cared for,
  - to be accepted unconditionally, just like he/she is,
  - to be sure that the ties of family affection are permanent.

We should communicate to each member of the family that there is nothing that they can do which would cause the loss of the ties of family affection. The poet Robert Frost[17] said that "home is the place that when you have to go there, they have to take you in." While this seems to be expressed from a rather cynical point of view, it has been true through the centuries, for the family and the home is the true setting of us all. One can be betrayed, disappointed, discouraged, estranged, embittered, hurt or saddened by a situation, but not bereft of family. Just knowing that "It's my mother," "It's my father," "It's my child," makes all the difference in the world. The significance of these basic relationships is still there. Even when there has been an estrangement in the relationship, roots of the affection remain, even though it is often denied.

Jesus demonstrates this aspect of family relationships in the parable that we call "The Prodigal Son." In the heartfelt and meaningful words of the loving father to the older brother, "Son, you are always with me, and all that is mine is yours. But we had to celebrate and rejoice, because this brother of yours was dead and has come to life, he was lost and has been found" (Luke 15:31-32). This is what it means to be a member of a family: loved, restored, and forgiven. The resolution of an estrangement is truly like a resurrection from the dead. It is a time of celebration.

4. The family's developmental needs must be met so that family equilibrium can be maintained. As needs are met and a new equilibrium is reached, this becomes the context in which the basic needs of the family are met. The family as an organization is not static, but dynamic; there is continuity as well as change in its status and relationships. The family that recognizes

that there is a constant need of change and adaptability is going to continue to grow and provide the basic foundational structure for life that each person needs.

5. When an individual member of the family does not have his/her basic developmental needs met it will be evidenced in symptoms of maladjustment. When this happens the family should reflect on the following questions:

   • In which developmental stage is the person at the present time?

   • How is the family helping the developmental process in this person?

On the basis of this reflection the family may find the key to the maladjustment of their family member and commit to help him/her meet the essential developmental needs for this stage in life.

The family is both a source and a resource of development for each of its members so that they can attain true personhood, becoming the person that God has ordained for His creation from the beginning. There is no other social nucleus with such a special responsibility as the family. Neither is there one that has greater possibilities of doing good or doing harm to its members. The family should make every effort to find and follow the paths that lead to healthy and meaningful relationships in order to carry out the high purpose given it by our loving Heavenly Father.

2. Basic theological beliefs about the family

Christians should not only base their understanding of the family on the concepts we have just mentioned, but also in their theological beliefs about the family. Every believer has his/her own theology, even though they may not have realized it. The Christian woman should have clear biblical concepts of the family and their underlying theological beliefs. The following are concepts that can give structure and meaning to the family and to each of its members:

1. God created the family:

   • In order to provide the setting for the most intimate form of companionship and love;

   • To provide a loving and stable setting where children could be born and raised in security and stability;

- To provide a nucleus where each member of the family could be protected and cared for.

2. Each person develops his/her basic identity in the family, developing there also the image of God in his/her life, although this can become distorted.

3. The family is the context in which the person is formed and where he/she develops their set of values.

4. The family is the cradle of the theology the person will have. It is in the family where the roots of the concept of God take hold.

5. The two psycho-social dynamics of the family are the force for unity and the force for individuality. These two forces should be maintained in equilibrium. That is to say, both of these forces should exist in a family, but each should function in a healthy way.

6. The evidence that the family is fulfilling the creative purpose of God is seen in their willingness and their capacity to sustain the self-differentiation of its members. Every member of the family is unique, different from all the rest. Many times it is hard to face the differences, but it is absolutely necessary that each person becomes his/her own self if he/she and the family are to be healthy and become what each was meant to be.

The family continues to be the most important institution in the development of the individual in their identity as a person and in the basic teaching of the theological concepts that should govern their life. The family is a great gift from God to help us live more meaningful lives during our entire life.

The mother's role in the family

Nearly all literature about the family emphasizes the role of the mother. Because of her unique role, she has the possibility of influencing every member of the family more than anyone else. The new creature to be born is formed in the body of the mother, she nourishes the child with her body and with her heart, she cares for his/her needs, and she is the child's first teacher, helping him/her find the right ways of doing things. As we have already seen women are nurturers and feel strongly about the importance of relationship between all members of the family. They work hard to maintain these relationships and to promote them among the other family members.

In spite of what we often hear on Mothers' Day, we know that mothers can also have a very negative influence in the life of their children. Eugenia Price[18], in a book about women, conducted some 250 interviews with both men and women about how the transforming power of Jesus Christ can change a life that was on the path to destruction. Among those interviewed, 212 said that they had either been blessed or cursed by their mothers. Unfortunately, more frequently it was to have been cursed rather than to have been blessed by this most important relationship!

It is not only the dominant mother who influences her child or other members of the family in this negative way. Frequently it is the complainer, the weepy mother, the one who is always worried about herself, the obsessive, the timid, or the neurotic mother who has the greatest influence in the life of the family members. It is a negative influence that remains engraved on the personality of the child throughout the remainder of his/her life. So as we can easily see the mother's influence is potentially powerful, either for blessing or for harming the child or the children in her home.

One of the most important needs of every person is to become an individual, a person who is distinct from others. To achieve this, we need to be able to differentiate ourselves from others. The mother, more than the father, has the tendency to fuse her relationship with her child. This is found especially when the mother relates to the child from an emotional perspective and fuses the child to her emotionally.

Emotions should not control our lives.

Every individual has the capacity to function both intellectually or cognitively as well as emotionally. While these two capacities need to be maintained separately in their particular function, there must be a basic harmony between the two. If these capacities are maintained separately but in harmony one with the other, there is the possibility of controlling them and to choose between the two, seeking the most appropriate function for each situation. If the two are united or "fused", the person will be controlled by his/her emotions. No longer is choice available to them for they are controlled by their emotions. This fact brings disastrous consequences to everyone involved.

This does not mean that our emotions are bad, but that they should not control our lives. The healthy person has both emotions and sentiments; these inform his/her thoughts and conduct, but they do not control them. The person with a healthy, well-balanced personality can be affected by his/her emotions, take them into consideration, and still make rational decisions for his/her life.

When a person is controlled by anxiety, there is more probability of fusion with another person. This can be seen in the lack of differentiation between the two and the absence of a true individuality in each person. In this situation the person does not act freely, but is controlled, manipulated, and used. The result is traumatic for the whole family.

There are certain "red flags" of warning that we as mothers should take into account that can help us save ourselves, our families and each family member. The following relational "red flags" should demand our attention:

- Recognition that we are controlling other members of our family,

- Recognition that we are being controlled by our emotions,

- Recognition that we have problems with members of the family either in their dependence on us or the possibility of a rupture of our relationship,

- Recognition that members of our family have not developed their personhood as individuals, STOP!

We need to stop and take time to give serious attention to our family and our role in the family. We need to look for help in promoting healthier relationships. Psychological studies of families that have problems such as those indicated above indicate that these unhealthy patterns continue from generation to generation. If there are fusion and unhealthy relations in the family, it is passed on to the children, and to their children, and on and on in succeeding generations. As mothers we must promote physical and emotional health not only for ourselves, but also for every member of our family. In doing so, we will bless not only our children, but our grandchildren, our great-grandchildren and those who follow them. Truly we have a power and influence that is great beyond measure!

As we grow in our own self-differentiation we will be able to give ourselves to our family in ways that can truly bless them. Our actions will be based on our intellectual, rather than our emotional and controlling functioning. As a result, each one will be able to see him/herself as an individual, a separate, distinct person, blessed by an understanding and healthy family.

The woman who knows what she believes, who understands her role in life, who has a well-defined scale of values, who is willing to pay the price for her self-differentiation, is going to be able to give her family the great benefit of guidance without controlling or manipulating them. Instead, she will be building an environment in which each member of the family can become a distinct individual. "Her children rise up and bless her" will also be the experience of this woman.

The family's heritage

The heritage we receive from our parents and pass on to our children is of incalculable value. There is always a family heritage, even though there may not be an inheritance of great or small economic value. There is the heritage of our attitudes, our ways of doing things, our values, our religious beliefs, our formation as a person and how we have lived our lives.

Several years ago at Christmas time I wrote a small tract about the importance of the gifts that we can give our children; gifts that would truly be a heritage that would help the child grow in their formation as a person. I repeat it here because I believe that it continues to have great value for the family. These are gifts that go beyond the normal Christmas gift, though those are given with much love and many times with great sacrifice and meaning. The gifts listed here will last a lifetime and will help define a child's life.

What Can I Give My Child?

It's always a good time to give a gift to your child – birthdays, Christmas, or some other special occasion. We take great care in buying just the right gift even though it may "stretch our budget," for we want our child to be pleased.

However, we know that the doll will break, the book will be torn, the car will lose its wheels, and the dress will get stained and become too small, but what about a giving a gift that lasts? What about a gift that will become a functional and stable heritage for your child, something that will last for a lifetime? Let's consider some of these gifts:

1. **Love.** Without a doubt love is the greatest gift a parent can give a son or daughter - sustaining love, active and dynamic love, pardoning love, unconditional love. A good daily exercise for every mother and father is to say to your child, (and to mean it!), "I love you," and to show this love in all your dealings with him/ her.

2. **Acceptance.** Every person is different from every other person. Why do we try to mold the child into being like his/her sibling, or like some make-believe child that is completely foreign to the family's reality? Accept your

child as he/she is. Feel strongly about his/her value as a person. Inspire her/him by your attitude toward their finding self-fulfillment.

3. **Discipline.** Parents must discipline their children, not rigidly and with an exaggerated authority, but with understanding, so that the child may know what is expected of him/her and the limits placed on him/her. Parents should agree on the discipline of their children, so that the child will not be confused nor see opportunities to manipulate the parents because of the lack of agreement on their part. The purpose of the parent's discipline is to prepare the child to be ready for self-discipline during his/her youth and adulthood. Discipline is not the same as punishment; discipline is to instruct, to teach, to put life on the right track.

4. **A clear idea of the role of men and women.** The child learns what it is to be a man or a woman in the home, and the two most important teachers for him/her are the parents. If in your family one of the parents is missing, or if the couple lives together but are constantly fighting, the child will receive a distorted concept of his/her role and that of the opposite sex that will make it difficult or impossible to function well as an adult.

5. **Communication.** There is a great need for understanding between children and their parents. Communication is more that dialogue; it is to talk, but it is also to listen and to understand. You can communicate with a smile, a hug, with compassion and empathy, and by putting yourself in the situation of the other person. Communication begins when the child is born, but even in situations where the relationship has been broken, with dedication and effort you can open the way to communicate again.

6. **Honesty.** Every child should have the security of knowing that his/her parents are honest and speak truthfully. Boys and girls, even when they are small, know, and feel it deeply, when their parents are not telling the truth. For this reason many young people do not trust their parents, and they themselves are dishonest, having learned from their parents that it is the "natural" and "easy" thing to do.

7. **Companionship.** Every child should consider him/herself a part of the family. They should have the experiences of going out with the family, of a family picnic, to sing and play together, to discuss a problem together, These family experiences are the memories that will help give them stability in the future.

8. **Example of maturity.** Parents should not behave as children. They should continue learning, studying, developing so that they can live as mature and responsible persons in the family and in society. The child should expect and receive the example of growing maturity in his/her parents.

9. **Independence.** Every child has to learn to become independent. Parents, both mother and father, have the responsibility to teach the child from the early years gradual independence and personal responsibility. As the child gets older, he/she receives more independence and responsibility until they are ready to get a job, marry, and establish themselves in the community.

10. **Faith in God.** Parents should share their beliefs with their children. There are parents that say, "I am going to wait for my child to decide about religious matters when he/she is older. I don't want him/her to be prejudiced in any way by my beliefs." Such at attitude only teaches the child that matters of faith are not important for their parent. However, children need faith, they need to know God and about God, and they need to internalize the moral teachings that are a part of faith. This they will learn best in the setting of the home through the daily lives and authentic commitment of their parents.

The world needs men and women of faith, people with moral and spiritual convictions, and the individual needs these convictions in order to live a life that is meaningful and full. Faith in God is learned in the home. Leaving this responsibility exclusively to the church is to harm the moral structure of the child, and later of the adult.

What are you going to give your child? Why not some of these ten gifts - every day? What a gift that will be! What a heritage for a child!

A word of caution ... be careful!

Paul gives a word of caution, or we might even say a cry of caution, about the treatment of children by their parents. "Fathers, do not provoke your children, or they may lose heart." NRSV; "Fathers, do not embitter your children, or they will become discouraged" NIV; (Colossians 3:21.) This is a very important word and should be listened to with a great deal of attention by both parents. It is easy to discourage a child when we constantly yell at him/her, or when we give contradictory messages of our love and our care for the child. Many children fear their parents because they have been mistreated by them, physically, emotionally or verbally. Such a situation leads the child to lose heart and to be come discouraged. A good father and a good mother will not treat their child in this way; rather they will encourage the child with love and acceptance.

One of the great evils of our times is the mistreatment and abuse of children. The sad truth is that usually this mistreatment is done to children by their families. This is brought about by the combination of different factors, including the violence and evil in the world, the frustrations and tensions in our agitated lives, the patterns of conduct that use and manipulate other persons, and a misguided sense of power over those who are more vulnerable. Without a doubt this problem is growing and we as Christian parents must do all we can to combat the destruction of children's lives, including those of our own children. Our child is not our possession to be treated as a "thing," or to be mistreated physically and emotionally. He/she is our offspring and has been given to us by God, and we are responsible for his/her integral formation. Facing such a responsibility the words of Paul take on an incalculable value: "And you, fathers, do not provoke your children to anger, but bring them up in the discipline and instruction of the Lord" (Ephesians 6:4).

The words of our Lord, "In this you will know that you are My disciples, if you have love one for the other" (John 13:35), give a vision for our conduct in and outside the family unit.

There are parents who do not consider their children as persons, rather as things, as their own possession. As a result they think that they can treat the child however they wish. Children are not the possession of their families; in truth they have been placed in the care of the parents by God. He has given the parents of every child the responsibility for their formation, their development, their life. One very important task for the father and mother is to study the temperament and the personality of the child so as to find the way in which this child should go, the education that is best suited for him/her, then "even when he/she is old, they will not depart from it" (Proverbs 22:6).

One of the biblical helps for being sure that our children are on the right path to becoming who they were meant to be is found in Deuteronomy 6:1-9. These words of instruction show God's use of multiple means to help the parents live their faith daily, to learn and follow the teachings of the Bible, along with the willingness to use every "teachable moment" to share their faith is the most meaningful way for the formation of their son or daughter. Such an appropriate education will permit the child to have a healthy and significant relationship with God during their childhood and throughout the rest of their lives.

Another great help is to have a good sense of humor; good for both parents and their children. The ability to laugh at oneself, to not take everything, even the most insignificant daily event, so seriously, will help tremendously in the interpersonal relationships of the family. The family home should be one of love and happiness. It should be a haven for all its members and a setting in which each person finds encouragement, rest and renewal.

Mothers should do all they can to assure that there is good communication in the family. We need to learn to speak with clarity, to say what we want and need to say, and learn to listen intently. We should learn to have good verbal communication and understand well the non-verbal communication that frequently is the more important of the two. The way in which we communicate with our child is just as important as the way in which we communicate with our spouse. Don't forget that you child is being formed "right before your eyes." He/she needs to communicate with you in ways that are significant to him as well as to you.

I remember when my older daughter was about nine or ten years old. I was in the kitchen, very busily preparing dinner. She was talking with me, and I was "half-listening," responding with grunts of "um," "ah-um" which we emit when we have our minds occupied in something else. After a few minutes my daughter tugged at my apron and said, "Mommy, I want you to listen to me with your eyes." She taught me a great truth that day: good communication requires our complete attention; it must be active, never passive.

This word of caution: being attentive to how we relate to our children is of great importance to every Christian mother. Don't ignore it; listen to it, reflect on it, and make the necessary and most appropriate decisions to see that your communication with your child/ren is all that it should be.

I am a woman. I am special in my relationship with my family as a mother. With a better idea of the family and role of the mother, there is no doubt that the heritage I help form for my children will be more what God wants for them and for me. Knowing and affirming who I am as a person made in God's image will help me be strong as I face this great responsibility and be the mother that my family really needs.

Activities for reflection and learning

1. Reflect on your relationship with your mother, noting one positive and one negative thing that you have received from her. As an adult, try to understand each aspect and if you have the opportunity, talk to your mother about your reflection. If you have resentments with her, perhaps this might be the moment to clarify them, and ask for and give forgiveness one to the other, and thus enter into a new relationship with each other.

2. Write a paragraph in which you describe "The Mother I Want to Be". Consider and reflect about the teachings of this chapter as you write.

3. Note three values that you want your children to learn in the home. Why have you chosen these? What can you do so that your children will assimilate your set of values? Be specific in your answers.

4. Make a study of Genesis 25:19-34 and 27:1-28:9, noting the role of the mother in these accounts. Note both the positive and the negative actions taken by the mother and the effect these actions have had in the life of the children in this family.

Questions to answer alone or in a group

• Briefly define the family, perhaps even in one word.

• What are the basic responsibilities of the family?

• In what ways can a mother bless her family?

• In what ways can a mother curse or punish her family? As a Christian woman how can you bring healing to your family in such a situation?

8. As a Woman in the Different Stages of Life

> *See what love the Father has given us, that we should be*
> *called children of God; and that is what we are....*
> *Beloved, we are God's children now;*
> *what we will be has not yet been revealed. What we do*
> *know is that when He is revealed, we will be like Him...*
> *whoever says, "I abide in Him," ought to walk*
> *just as He walked. John 3:1, 2; 2:6*

Generally women develop in the context of their families. Since their basic orientation as a person is that of relationships with a sense of responsibility for others, they will maintain family ties almost at any cost to themselves.

Although this is the need or the basic orientation of women, we have different basic needs in the different stages of our lives. As women, we need to be very conscious of this reality so that we may live each stage in ways that will make our development most significant and abundant.

Women's development in the different stages of life

One of the most important helps for studying the development of the individual is to recognize the different developmental tasks for each stage of life. Developmental tasks are the responsibilities that every person must fulfill in each stage before passing on to the successive stage. The chart "The Cycle of Family Life" can help you understand this process in the life of the family, beginning with the marriage and continuing until the death of the spouses. In each stage the tasks are different, the challenge is that these tasks be fulfilled before passing on to the next stage.

THE CYCLE OF FAMILY LIFE[19]

Stage	Developmental Tasks for the Family
	(These are limited to the immediate family; the developmental tasks of the parents)
I. From marriage to the birth of the first child	Movement from the role of individuals to that of a couple. Movement from the idealistic expectations of spouse to a realistic appreciation of the person.
II. From birth of first child to their entry in school	Movement from the role of a couple to that of parents. Upbringing of child. Responding to needs and interests for optimal development.
III. Period of Elementary School	Helping child begin well in educational environment. Maintaining responsibility for child
IV. Period of Adolescence	Establishing a balance between distance and emotional closeness as child enters puberty. Developing interests outside the home.
V. Period of "Letting Go"	Permitting and facilitating the young person to leave home, begin college or work. Helping young adults move from partial dependence to responsible independence.

The concept of developmental tasks in the context of the family is of great importance because it takes into account the need to work toward the development of certain relationships and activities which many people take for granted, as if they are events that will happen without effort. Without this concerted effort many of the problems and tensions in the family will be exacerbated, and the health of the family will be compromised.

Women have basic needs and interests with their corresponding developmental tasks in each stage of her life. These should be recognized by her and by her family. The young woman experiences emotional and psychological tensions that can be very pronounced as she enters into marriage. She faces the separation from the family into which she was born and the formation of a new relationship with her husband simultaneously. Even though our society praises separation, autonomy and individualization, the young adult woman is pushed and pulled by separation from her birth family on the one hand toward that of joining her life with a new person on the other. Her husband-to-be does not suffer this same struggle for it is natural for him to seek separation and he defines himself as a person as he forms this new relationship. The woman, on the other hand, is searching for a relationship that creates and sustains a sense of community. An understanding of these basic differences can help the couple to overcome many of the problems that will be faced in marriage, especially in the first months and years.

When a woman is asked to define who she is, she does so through her relationships: "mother-to-be," "wife of _____," "mother of _____," "daughter of _____," and other forms which always emphasize her relationships. One can observe a group of young women professionals who have achieved a certain degree of success in their work who will still describe themselves through their relationships with their family or their work. Women in every stage of life will continue to emphasize their desire to give themselves to others, to help others, to be considerate of others, to be kind to others, to not cause problems or hurt to others. There continues to be a struggle between being able to reconcile the relationship of their professional life and activity with that of their personal sense of identity.

To understand this aspect of women's life, one must remember the great need for relationship, affiliation, and belonging. It is much greater than that seen in men's development. Little girls play being a mother, a teacher, a nurse, or other forms of nurturing and relating to others - all caring and relating roles. The young woman wants a boy friend who calls her frequently, who is aware of how she dresses and cares for herself, who takes her out so they can be together, who is perhaps the one with whom she can share her life. The young mother seeks to establish relationships that will be life-long with her children. Her need to live in relationship can push her toward unhealthy relationships as we have seen previously. It is very difficult for a mother to see her children leave home when it is time for them to go to college, or to enter the workforce.

Sometimes a mother will make the decision that her children must not leave home, and she does all she can to prevent this step, causing great harm to everyone involved.

When the relationship with her husband is not going well, the wife suffers a great deal. The relationship to which she has given her whole life is ending. Many women see in this broken relationship not just the loss of the relationship, but something even larger, the total loss of herself, of who she is as a person.

If the wife has considered that her principal value as a person is in her ability to bear children, when she goes through menopause she will feel that she no longer has any value. If she is isolated from her family and feels completely alone, she will have even more reason to believe her worthlessness. She will begin to think that she is getting old, and will probably die before too long. She is going through a period of grief for herself that results in melancholy and depression. And so the events leading to middle age reflect the interaction between the reality of life and the workings of her imagination and thoughts.

But if the middle-aged woman, or an older woman, has someone with whom she can relate positively, her perspective can be changed totally. Rather than being depressed and thinking of dying, she thinks of living longer, of being a vital part of life and, especially in that of her family. For this reason the church can have an important role to play in the life of women, not only in their spiritual lives, but also psychologically and emotionally. They can be given opportunities to relate with children, with young people and with other adults. They can become tutors for children who are not doing well in school; they can become an adopted grandmother to a child with problems, or with one who doesn't have a grandmother nearby. Also, they can participate in meaningful activities with people of their own age. All these are experiences of great value for women in this stage of their lives.

Women find that interdependence is a very important aspect of relationship. They do not want to be dependent as they were in their childhood and youth, nor independent as in adolescence or as is seen many times in men, but women want interdependence. This is a relationship of love, a more human relationship. It is one that will last. This type of relationship must have been formed and structured in their lives for years to really work well in their more advanced years, but it is never too late to begin a new relationship, or to give a new sense of relationship to one that already exists.

I read of a woman who was seventy-five years old when she became a Christian. As a result she was beginning to have a new sense of relationship with her husband. She was aware that she had lost many opportunities to relate lovingly to him through the years, but rather than lamenting the past she focused on changing and improving the relationship and finding new ways of expressing the importance of the new relationship they were forming. She had found new life for both her spiritual relationship with God and for her marital relationship with her husband!

The middle-aged woman comes to this stage in life with a sense of value and experiences different from that of men. Because of the childbearing and nurturing functions of her body, she recognizes innately how different she is from men. She cannot completely control her life; her autonomy and control are relative. These realities are something that men have to learn and appreciate for their own lives when they, too, are middle-aged. Sometimes it is just too hard to reach this goal. However, the way in which a woman's life has developed points the way not only to a less violent life, but to a maturity that comes into being as a result of interdependence and care of others. Understanding this asset can give new meaning to the life of the couple and their family.

Interdependence is a very important aspect of relationship.

One of the basic problems for understanding the differences in our development as men and women is that we "talk" in two different languages. However, we must learn to listen carefully to each of these two languages. An open dialogue about rights and justice, care and responsibility, is going to produce better relations between the two and a better understanding of adult life both in the family as well as in their individual development. Such an understanding is not attained in one exchange, but must be an on-going aspect of marital and family life.

The adult's life is even more complicated, for both men and women have had huge losses during their lifetime. Recognizing this truth will give you an excellent criterion for understanding reactions and actions of your spouse, as well as your own. For our study here we will look at the situations where adult women face a special loss, especially one that threatens her basic need of relation with others.

The losses in all aspects of life cause the adult woman to expend enormous amounts of physical and emotional energy as she attempts to adapt to these changes. Some of these losses are:

• Loss as a result of the death of her husband, parents, friends, colleagues, and possibly children. These losses are constant reminders that she must face the reality of death as well as life.

* The loss or decline of her health.

* The loss of her position, status, and prestige in society, as well as her meaningful participation in social activities.

* The loss of her lifestyle; feeling that she is a burden to others, in many ways to live marginalized from the activities that she participated in previously.

* The loss of social relationship: social collapse or social death brought on as a result of constantly internalizing her marginalization and thus her sense of inferiority in relation to others.

Together with these losses the older adult must find new ways of adapting to these changes. Rarely do we take into consideration the challenge facing the older adult woman to find ways in which she must adapt to the accelerated changes in her life, her sentiments and her context. As in all new learning, there is anxiety in proportion to the task. Frequently this anxiety and its expressions are seen as an evidence of "old age" and considered to be a form of incurable ageing and even dementia, but we must be very careful with such a diagnosis. The older adult can be anxious or confused when he/she is faced with learning or adapting to something new as a result of internalizing the alienating and marginalizing way he/she is treated by others. It is a deadly characterization imposed on the older adult by society.

We know that the older adults can learn, can change, can be creative, can help others, and can make the life of others more meaningful and significant. The older adult may do things a bit more slowly than others, but he/she is more conscientious about the task at hand, and many times will do it better than younger persons. In a study done over a period of twenty years in classes of creativity training, people over forty years of age took maximum advantage of the course, improving their effectiveness in their workplace more than double than those who were less than thirty years old. In addition, the creative ideas that were useful and workable that resulted from the class had come from those over forty years old. Adults can learn, and adults do learn. An adult learns things he/she is interested in and things that he/she needs to make life better.

Contradictory to common thinking, the older adult does not have to deteriorate mentally or cognitively. The brain does not diminish but rather continues to function normally even into their nineties and beyond. Less that one percent of adults over seventy years of age suffer dementia. Although brain cells are lost, and these cannot be replaced, they are not necessary! We have an over supply of brain cells that permit the older adult to have this normal loss, and still be able to function well, as we see in the lives of so many older adults in our families and communities..

Many gerontologists believe that the reason why older adults deteriorate is because of the way in which they are treated, the verbal and non-verbal messages they receive, such as "you can't do this," "you're too old," "you're old-fashioned," "you don't understand anything," and others just as hurtful and debilitating. As a result the older adult begins to believe these constant messages, to feel that they are true, and thus to become what he/she has been accused of. Thus they lose hope, and as a result life ends in dislocation, disorientation, or death. Even the well-meaning, "You've worked all your life. You deserve a good rest now," can keep older adults from engaging in meaningful activities that would enhance their lives.

In experimental studies done in the University of Denver a psychologist was able to induce signs of advanced dementia in some volunteers who were twenty to thirty years of age.[20] These signs began to be seen a few hours after beginning the experiment in which they were being ignored constantly, their ideas were considered to be without value, and they were told that they did not have any function in society. So, too, the older adult can be influenced by negative stereotypes that make normal functioning impossible. As a society and as a family we must do all we can to destroy the use of these stereotypes and emphasize the value of a person in all the stages of their lives. Today we see an increasing number of people in different parts of the world who live and function into advanced age, their nineties and beyond. The most rapidly increasing demographic worldwide is the number of adults over the age of eighty, going from 13 million people in 1950, to 1990 more than 50 million, and it is estimated that by 2025 the number will have grown to be 137 million![21]

Young and middle-aged women must form relationships with older women, seeking to enhance the life of an older woman they know, to value her capacity for relationship, her knowledge gained from her long life, and her continued zest for life. Older women must take heart and find hope for their lives and their relationships. They must know that they are women of great value. At the same time they need to relate both to people of their own age as well as those who are younger. They can become adoptive grandmothers to a child, they can teach others what they have learned through their long lives, they can become fellow partners in the pilgrimage of life with both younger and older people. Life is not over for the older adult, it still can be meaningful and significant.

Sarah Patton Boyle, in her marvelous book, *The Desert Blooms,*[22] based on her personal experiences facing ageing following an unanticipated divorce, speaks of the importance of living in what she calls "the eternal today." She had been in a time of severe depression when she heard a disabled man say that one could face any problem if they did so in the present moment. One must live in the present!

Sarah remembered passages from the Bible, "Do not remember the former things, or consider the things of old. I am about to do a new thing; now it springs forth; do you not perceive it?!" (Isaiah 43:18, 19a)

Years later Paul said, "Beloved, I do not consider that I have made it my own, but this one thing I do, forgetting what lies behind and straining forward to what lies ahead, I press on toward the goal for the prize of the heavenly call of God in Christ Jesus" (Philippians 3:13, 14.) And Christ told us in the Sermon on the Mount, "So do not worry about tomorrow, for tomorrow will bring worries of its own. Today's trouble is enough for today" (Matthew 6:34).

Sarah continues saying,

> "Again and again, the Bible points to the eternal now. Yet I had been plodding on, dragging yesterday after me and staggering under the weight of tomorrow. Incidents that hurt, angered or frightened me drew much of their dark power from associations of memories or anticipations. Painful experiences just encountered, injustices just endured, mistakes just made, opportunities just lost, and failures just scored pushed crucial current issues from my mind. Probably not more than 2 or 3 percent of my thoughts focused sharply on present reality. And inadequacy, failure and defeat were the heavy interest I paid on my borrowed trouble.

> "Now, I realized that only the present can be acted in. Problems of the past and future can only be reviewed, worried over, circled around and around. Good memories can be refreshing, and bad ones can be learned from. But, good or bad, when memories hamper present functioning, it is time to turn them out. There is a place for pondering the future, when present actions or decisions can altar its outcome. But when tomorrow appears only as an instrument of destruction, anxiety alone results.

"Focusing on the present is not an easy discipline. But as an awareness of the eternal now worked its magic in my consciousness, the world around me began to sparkle and shine. I perceived sunlight in a different way. Flowers, trees, clouds, the richly varied music of nature and of man rounded out and became full. Friends appeared more vibrant, pristine, alive. I was more aware of myself. Longing, timidity, hope, appreciation, anger, joy and gratitude moved visibly inside me. A new dimension expanded my consciousness of stars, moon, warmth of fire and bracing sting of wind. Nature's abundance and variety burst upon me with a shock. In my muscle and marrow, I felt the sometimes hastening, sometimes plodding energy of all living things.

"Above all, I felt the overwhelming majesty of God and my own dependence on Him. The world of the present is the one that God makes. Our images of our yesterdays and tomorrows are our own handiwork. We choose to live in the dull, dim, aching, unreal worlds we make, instead of in Eden. By that choice we bring upon ourselves exile."[23]

As we have said from the beginning, women usually develop in relationship with the family. Our developmental tasks for each stage of life demand great integrity, having a clear sense of our identity and value as a person, and having ample opportunities to develop significant relationships with others. Women must recognize the importance of their own way of development and make it their way of life. In doing so they can also grow toward becoming the woman God has intended them to be.

The family plays a decisive role in each stage of life. It can facilitate and collaborate in the development of its female family members, or it can hamper and divert their development, causing trauma and keeping them from their realization as a person. Seek the collaboration and the help of your family in each stage of your life. Together with them, you will be able to emphasize, "I'm a woman, I'm special."

A clear concept of your identity

One of the most important developmental tasks for every person is to have a clear concept of their identity. Although our identity is rooted in childhood, it is a precise task of adolescence to bring about a convergence of the different elements of our identity into an accepted framework for life. If it is not achieved, the result will be confusion of our role in life and as we enter into adulthood we will be uncertain about our identity, and our life will be affected in every area. Instead of being a person who can develop life to its potential, based on the right concepts of our abilities and interests, we will be in doubt about who we are, going from one concept to another, and constructing a life that is constantly in turmoil. The struggle will continue until our true identity is understood and becomes a part of all that we are as an individual.

In the past women did not experience the difficulty of knowing who they were to such an extent as today because society dictated their roles and identity and most women accepted these dictates without question. Today, however, with so many rapid social changes women have less certainty about their role and identity, and how to affirm the concept of their identity. This book is an effort to speak to this need and to help Christian women know and appreciate themselves as made in God's image and likeness with all the blessings that brings to their life and their identity.

In her book *Identity*, Dr. Ruth Tiffany Barnhouse[24] emphasizes the idea that in order to find one's identity as a person, there are four premises that must be considered by women. These four will be listed and then these ideas will be developed for our study.

1. "She must recognize the advantage of the old ways and be willing either to give them up or to pay the price for retaining them,

2. She must eradicate not only the conscious but the unconscious belief in male supremacy,

3. She must recognize the specifically feminine qualities of her consciousness and learn to value them appropriately,

4. She must realize that to find *herself* is not, and never can be, a betrayal of relationship with others."

Many women who believe in the total "liberation" of women unconsciously still want men to assume responsibility for them! It is important to understand the motive behind this desire. They have never seen, nor have shared experiences in mutual responsibility with men, and so they feel incapable of facing the possibility of "total liberation" for themselves. Faced with this situation, it is necessary to develop a model for women's identity that is in accord with her psychological structure, and one that does not sacrifice either her sense of responsibility or her need of relationship with others. We need to remember that the basic needs of women are for affiliation and attachment. It is vital that women recognize the controlling power of their unconscious attitudes about their self-concept and their role in life. Only when there is a congruence of attitudes and actions can we truly affirm our identity.

Social changes, including changes brought about by "feminine liberation" and/or the rising socio-political status of women in most of the world, have greatly influenced women's lives, although there are discrepancies many times between the ideals engendered by these changes and the way in which change and liberation have been carried out. While one recognizes that for this new modality to function it must be accepted by and adjusted to by women, at the same time we must remember that men have to adjust to this new situation also. These changes have brought great pressures to bear on them. For centuries in most societies men have been in control and women found their identification in their relationship to them. Many men have found it hard to adjust to this new status of women, especially from an intergenerational point of view. It is a difficult period for both men and women, and it is important to recognize and try to understand its reality and its implications.

The idea of the superiority of man is very common in society; a belief and a reality found in most cultures. It is as common as the air we breathe. However, many people who reject this idea intellectually believe it emotionally. They believe that men can do whatever they please, that they are privileged in the home, in society and in the workplace. They believe that they have the best jobs, have more prestige in their profession, receive a higher remuneration, are "in charge" of everything, and enjoy life more than women. More often than not it is women themselves that perpetuate these ideas!

There are many women who work all day outside of the home where they have positions of great responsibility in their professions and there are other women who choose to remain at home caring for their family, which they do in exemplary ways. However in both these cases, there are women who consider themselves to be second-class citizens. Unconsciously they believe that women are inferior to men and so they try as best they can "to be like Him", something that they will never achieve because of the basic differences between men and women and here, also, the power of their unconscious, internalized beliefs about the inferior status of women.

There are stereotypes for the roles of men and women, and when either steps outside of this stereotypical mold they are considered different and strange. Often there is the idea that men do valuable work, while the work of women is trivial. How often a housewife will say, "I don't work," or that is said of her, thus devaluating her life and the decision she has made to be a full-time housewife and mother. Women, and hopefully men, are aware of the hard work required of a "stay-at-home Mom:" caring for the children, cleaning the house, managing the household, buying and preparing food, keeping clothing clean and ready to wear, healing hurts both physical and emotional, among so many other aspects of her daily life.

While the traditional work carried on by women is oftentimes unappreciated, even by women themselves, many unconsciously think that the reason they have gotten some particular employment is because it is something men would not do, thus believing this work, and themselves, to be lacking of real value. This viscous circle of rejection of one's value as a worker produces a constant state of instability and self-disregard. We must break these chains that bind both men and women to such destructive attitudes and emphasize the importance of replacing them with self-appreciation and a healthy self-concept on the part of each, and in the way the other is seen and appreciated.

It will continue to be very difficult for women to have self-confidence in the distinctly feminine style they bring to the task they have been given unless they learn to value themselves as competent and put aside the tendency to consider men as superior only because they are men. If they achieve this understanding never again will they feel that their work is inferior to how a man would have done. Rather they will sense their value as a person who is capable of doing things in their own way. They will see themselves as persons who have contributed to the restoration of a healthy balance between men and women in their personal relationship, and even extending to the world.

The interest that women have in affiliation, attachment, and maintaining relationships with other persons frequently will keep them from taking advantage of the personal advances that have been achieved for women in many areas of life. However, her orientation toward relationships is precisely one of the most valuable assets that women bring to our hostile and needy world.

Women can never deny their basic orientation toward maintaining valued relationships and the importance of their responsibility in them. Nevertheless, they must recognize that there are relationships that do not meet these criteria.

Not all relationships are equal in depth, quality or importance. It is necessary to differentiate among our relationships in order to decide which are valued and should be preserved. In addition women should avoid the excessive effort, so common in our midst, to maintain the happiness of everyone among her relationships whatever the cost may be to themselves, and often to others as well. Rather than producing a healthy relationship these activities produce dependence, resentment and frustration.

The woman who has established her own identity and has chosen well the relationships which are to be maintained can be confident in the sincerity and continuity of these relationships, for they are genuine. Thus she will not need to waste her energy trying to maintain the happiness of everyone, but rather she can cultivate relationships that are of special importance for her. The task of finding and developing our identity is essential to a woman's growth as a person. It must continue during each stage of our life because our identity is not developed in a day, rather it is a constant and necessary process that can lead to a life of significance and realization.

Dr. Barnhouse[25] suggests four techniques that can help women develop a more authentic sense of identity. I believe they are valuable for us to follow.

1. "**Magical Wishes**: If you could have three magical wishes, what would they be? Before reading further, ask yourself that question and make a note of your answers.

   1st wish _____

   2nd wish _____

   3rd wish _____ "

   Women frequently wish for things that will benefit another person, rather than imagining something that might be only for themselves. "Once women know what they want *for themselves*, it is time enough to work out whether or not it is possible to pursue that goal while keeping other people's needs in mind. Practice this 'magical wish' exercise until you can easily think of three things for yourself, and make at least one of them come true without a twinge of guilt!"

2. **Imagination.** This is a type of "planned daydream." Many times women are completely limited by the stereotypes given by society that leave little option for her. For this exercise it is necessary to imagine yourself

assuming a different role with others in which you emphasize your value as a capable person. Using your imagination in this way, you can begin to have a different model or experience that can be used in the future in a real situation.

3. **Assertiveness Training**. Workshops on assertiveness training can be very helpful. Some women stay away from them because they confuse "assertiveness" with "aggressiveness" and fear that someone is going to try to teach them to be nasty! This is not the point. Such workshops give opportunities for women to practice standing up for themselves appropriately, learning to express their true opinions without giving offense.

4. **Counseling**. "If in spite of your best efforts with these techniques (or with others you may invent for yourself) you continue to have difficulty, some personal counseling may be in order. Many women shy away from that, fearing that to need counseling means something is seriously wrong with them. On the contrary. If you enjoyed swimming, wanted to do it better, but found that when you tried to dive all you could do was make a horrible splash, you would not feel badly about taking a few lessons from a swimming coach. This is really exactly the same."

Try these four techniques and use them to strengthen and expand the concept you have of your identity. As we develop in the different stages of our lives there are different challenges that we meet. Having a healthy sense of self-identity will be one of our most important assets as we face these challenges.

It is truly important for us to recognize that we are women in the process of development throughout the various stages of our lives. Each one of us has capabilities, needs, and developmental tasks to consider in each stage. Finding and affirming our own identity, and knowing clearly who we are, are important steps toward considering ourselves as women of true value in our families. To be valued as the person you are will enable you to rejoice in the relationships you have with each member of your family and with others. Truly you will be living your "specialness"!

Activities for reflection and learning

1. Describe the person you hope to be in five years, in fifteen years, and in twenty-five years. Are there changes you will need to make to achieve these goals?

2. What is the most important developmental task for you to meet at the present ?

   What are your plans to meet this goal? Can the techniques seen above help you in meeting these goals?

3. What is the age of your parents? Describe your relationship with them. Has the relationship changed because of their age? Because of your age? Because of the age of your children? Reflect on how you can improve this relationship.

4. Study 2 Kings 4:8-37; 8:1-6 noting the development of the life of the Sunamite woman in her relationship with her family, with the prophet, and with God. What specific lesson can you apply to your life from the experience of this woman?

Questions to answer alone or in a group:

- List two needs of women in each stage of her life: adolescence, young adult, middle-aged adult, older adult, and a very elderly woman. How are you filling or plan to fill these needs in your life? Are there decisions that you need to take as a result of the study of this chapter?

- What can you do to affirm your identity as a person? Write down several things you need to do, prioritizing them. How will you begin to put these into practice?

- How are the roles of different family members defined in your home? Do you feel that it would be better if everyone were more open and honest in making these definitions? Think of ways in which you can bring the possibility of this new relationship into being. Decide on one thing you can do and begin there. Continue as you work with your family to understand the division of roles and clarifications that need to be made.

- Describe how a healthy family changes through the years. Are there ways that you can prepare for these changes in your family that will make for a healthier, happier home?

9. As a Relational Change Agent

"Do not press me to leave you
or to turn back from following you!
Where you go, I will go; Where you lodge, I will lodge;
your people shall be my people, and your God my God.
Where you die, I will die – there will I be buried.
May the Lord do thus and so to me and more as well,
if even death parts me from you!" Ruth 1:16-17

Being a member of a family makes many demands on your life, especially when you are a woman/mother, but this is the context in which most women live, and it is where they will make their major contribution as relational change agents. The term "change agent" is found in sociology and is an important indicator of the fact that individuals produce change in their communities. There are change agents in every level of society, some working among a small circle of individuals and others in larger community settings, but in each change is sought and brought about by well thought-out plans. The change agent is a catalyst for the change that is planned for and produced.

In the development of this book, we have acknowledged women's commitment to relationship, and the importance of relationship in every aspect of her life. In combining these two concepts, that of the "change agent" and the importance of relationships we can speak of women as "Relational Change Agents." They recognize their value as women in relationship and they see the need for change in relationships in their family and in society. They can become catalysts as they promote relational change within the family and in society.

As women, we must see our role as active and not passive. We must not resign ourselves to the attitude of "What will be, will be," nor say, "There is nothing I can do to change the situation." Yes, women can do many things. They are the key persons who can promote a sense of family continuously.

The creativity of women, combined with their high sense of the importance of relationship and responsibility are valuable tools to achieve ever increasingly a happy family and one that is meaningful to all its members. In this chapter we will look at four specific contributions women can make as agents of relational change.

Promoting communication

Communication is essential for the family, but many families do nothing to promote communication among its members. In Christian and non-Christian families, communication is minimal, and many times exclusively with words and attitudes that are so negative that they hurt and wound rather than promote encounter and true communication.

To achieve good communication in our homes requires hard work. Without this effort, little will be achieved, for family communication is not an automatic phenomenon. The first step toward having good communication in your home is to want it sincerely. Then, you will be able to make a commitment with yourself and with your family that you will work together to improve your communication skills. Frequently you will need to remind yourself of this commitment because there will be times when you are discouraged and decide that it is not worth the effort to keep on trying.

What is good communication in the family? It is not constant talking or filling the room with superficial or cruel words. Communication is to reach the other person with a clear message, which he/she understands and then responds to with a message that is understood by the first person, to which he/she responds, continuing this "back and forth" until the communication is complete. Each person should participate expressing the words and the message he/she wants to share with the other. True communication is when the exchange includes both verbal expression and understanding. Communication is not, necessarily, being in agreement with the other person, but it is to listen to the message, to make the effort to understand it and to respond. There are times when a person will not hear, as if he/she were deaf, and this becomes an obstruction or a hindrance to communication. We must learn to know how to take advantage of the best opportunities, "the right moment", to engage in good communication in the family.

Women as relational change agents must learn how to be good communicators. They must learn how to express themselves clearly and sincerely. In order to do so a woman needs a good vocabulary that is understood by the members of her family. She needs to learn the language of sincere love that must be present in her communication day after day. At all times she must avoid dishonesty, insincerity, sarcasm and aggression. Communication that is based on dishonesty, insincerity or sarcasm will only alienate those with whom we want to communicate. An aggressive attitude will most likely produce a similar attitude in the other person, and eliminate the possibility of true communication. To be a relational change agent means that we will use our communication skills, including our sensitivity to other family members, to promote closer understanding and a more meaningful relationship in our families.

Communication is much more than just the exchange of words. We talk in non-verbal ways also. This includes gestures, movements of the eyes and body, silence, and the impact of the whole body, including the emotions and attitudes of the person. On many occasions we communicate verbally, but we contradict that message non-verbally. Interestingly, when there is this incongruent form of communication, we "hear" and believe the non-verbal message over the oral or verbal message. There are two ways of trying to solve this problem. First, stand before a mirror and practice conversations with others, noting and eliminating contradictory messages, gestures and movements that distract true communication. Second, ask a friend or a family member to tell you habits of non-verbal communication that you use continuously and are detrimental to what you are trying to communicate. We must have the maturity to accept these observations and determine to eliminate the habits that detract from maintaining good communication with our family and with others.

In order to be a good communicator, you must learn to listen attentively to what the other person is communicating. You must learn to listen actively, not looking at the floor, or the ceiling, or your watch; not moving continuously, rather giving your complete attention to the person and the communication at hand. When you do not understand what the person has said or manifested, or when you want more information, you must indicate that. Never be afraid to say, "Let me see if I have understood you correctly."

Sometimes in our families we can fall into the trap of thinking that the person always says the same thing and since we already know what he/she will say we cut off the communication by our attitude or by our words. The same process is often used with persons in whom we have little confidence in their truthfulness or their motivation. In our families we must make the effort always to "go the second mile" in order to better our relationships and our communication.

Our attitude toward the other person is vital in our communication. We must accept, respect, value, and believe in him or her. An adolescent commented that her father confused communication with giving advice. "He was always advising and counseling me, but when I asked him for his opinion about something that was important to me, he didn't answer me. To converse with my father is a one-way street, only his way."

Many times there are barriers between a mother and her children because when they are talking with her she is working on her make-up, or her jewelry, or her hair, things that can be very irritating to the person if they are trying to communicate with her. We must be careful with these habits for they not only frequently bring to an end the possibility of communication but also can cause rejection and resentment. We must treasure the moments of conversation we can have with our children and realize that time and attention must be given to them in every stage of their development.

I read many years ago that the dining table of the home should be a place for communication. "In a house there are many beds, but only one table." The table is a symbol of union and communion. Take advantage of the table as a setting for communication. Try to be sure that at least one time a day everyone is together at the table for a meal and for good conversation. "Do we talk enough?" is a question the family should ask itself daily, and if the response is negative, then they should investigate the reason for this and make a plan to begin to resolve this problem. If everyone doesn't participate or if only one person talks all the time, or if the subject matter is always about the same thing and using the same words, then truly there is no communication. You can be the key person to help your family look for ways of resolving this problem and to begin to communicate better and more openly.

The "Johari Window" is a great contribution to understanding each other better and to recognize the dynamics that make up true communication or human interaction. This is a window of the person and how each individual develops interpersonal communication and relationship. The window is divided into four panes or quadrants, each of which represents an aspect of the self-awareness of the person. Each pane reveals specific information, both from the viewpoint of the person as well as the viewpoint of others. The window offers a dynamic view of interpersonal communication, and changes in the distinct interpersonal relationships that are either revealed, hidden or unknown. A change in one area will signify a change in the other areas.

The Johari Window[26] is presented in the following way:

THE JOHARI WINDOW

		SELF	
		Known to Self	**Unknown to Self**
OTHERS	**Known to Others**	**1. OPEN** (**Known to self and others**)	**2. BLIND** (**Blind to self, seen by others**)
	Unknown to Others	**3. HIDDEN** (**Open to self, hidden from others**)	**4. UNKNOWN** (**Unknown to self and others**)

When I communicate with another person, my whole being, my total personality enters into the communication, including those parts of myself that I do not recognize or know. Since the majority of the relations each of us has are seen in Pane 1 of the individual's communicating, that is to say between the "Open Pane," of each, it is very important that this area be authentic. The larger the Open Pane is, the easier communication will be between the persons involved. As a result one of the important tasks of each person in meaningful and important communication is to enlarge the Open Pane. This is certainly true in relationships in the family.

As can be seen in the picture, there are two panes (numbers 1 and 3) that I know about myself. There are two panes (numbers 1 and 2) that others know about me. There are two panes (numbers 2 and 4) that I do not know about myself. There are two panes (numbers 3 and 4) that others do not know about me. There is one pane that I do not know about myself, but others know about me (number 2). There is one pane that I know about myself but others do not (number 3). And there is one pane that neither I nor they know (number 4).

The Johari Window not only can help us know ourselves better, but as we apply it in our communication with others it helps us to understand others better as well. Every time we enlarge Pane 1, either or both vertically and horizontally, we promote a more honest and open communication and self-awareness. At the same time as we communicate with others we can better understand ourselves and we become more aware of our "Hidden Selves" (Pane 3). In this way our self-awareness and our communication is strengthened and we are more prepared to establish better and more open relations with other persons.

In a study done in the Free University of Berlin entitled "The Behavior of Men and Women in Conversation"[27] it was shown that each uses a different style in conversation. "Men tend to distance themselves from the person with whom they are talking, while women, when they talk, create human ties. Men do not take this into consideration when they converse with others." These patterns demonstrate basic elements of the identity of each sex. Women take into consideration relationships in conversation. She is more involved in the conversation, and as she speaks she moves closer to the person than do men. On the other hand, men are prone to try to return to a more impersonal level with their interlocutor.

As women we have gifts that enable us to be good communicators and conversationalists. Let's use them to establish and maintain healthy relationships. Let's be relational change agents, stimulating and providing good communication in our families.

Eliminating barriers

There are many barriers to relationship that are present in our families that need to be eliminated. These barriers not only block our relationships with family members but they cause us to distance ourselves from them and as a result in many situations to break the ties of the relationship. **Lack of time** is one of the barriers that we experience in our agitated and rapidly moving world. There is not enough time to establish or to develop relationships. There are many things that take time from our families: our work, the long distances that separate us, the distinct schedules of family members, our commitments, and our hobbies, our recreation, and our pastimes. In many occasions the church can become a hindrance to family relationships when there is an excess of activities.

One of the things that robs the family of both time and relationship is the constant presence of the television in our homes. The hour of a favorite program - be it a sitcom, the next chapter in a "Soap Opera," a sports program, the news, or some other program - becomes the most important hour of the day. In many cases we become so involved in these programs that we know more about the participants and their activities than we do of our own family members. Not only is television a barrier to our family life as a result of the time and commitment involved, but also it becomes a social and moral barrier because of the lifestyle depicted in many of its programs. Instead of emphasizing positive Christian values that could give stability and significance to our lives, there is a sharp absence of values. In many programs attitudes that are most frequently presented are egocentric, negative and malicious. The advertisements not only present concepts and ways of life of the products being promoted, but they manipulate the person to strive for a certain image that frequently is far from family and Christian values.

We must be able to limit the time in which the television is on in our families so that we control the television rather than it controlling us. An important task for you as a mother is to help your children distinguish between propaganda and reality and between family life from a Christian point of view and that which is presented on television which frequently gives a distorted view of life.

We each are given twenty-four hours a day. It is a gift that we receive from our loving Heavenly Father. We need to consider carefully how this gift will be used in our families. Time spent with our children in the different stages of their lives is an essential part of our responsibility as mothers. It is time "well spent" and we will reap its dividends for years to come. Certainly the time spent with our children and other members of the family is one way in which the mother can exert her influence as a Relational Change Agent. Relationships established and developed will produce a firm foundation for life for years to come.

Another barrier to family relationship is the **fatigue** we experience in our contemporary lives, whether it be from work, school, or church activities, or from our desire to have just the right program of recreation. We must avoid being constantly in one activity or another that leaves us so fatigued that we come home only to rest. In such a setting it is impossible to develop good communication skills or meaningful relationships. We must make the effort to resist such an agitated and tiring lifestyle. As a relational change agent you can try to see that each person has adequate rest, including yourself, so that the family will be able to relate to one another in a more sincere and relaxed way.

Another modern day trap, and cause of our chronic fatigue, is to sit in front of the television in order to relax. This is not the best way to relax as we have already mentioned. As a relational change agent you can help your husband and other members of the family to have a time alone following a hard day of activity before they hear of the activities of other members of the family and participate in a time of family communication. Not only do the family members need this "time alone" but you do also. Our fatigue can rob us of our desire for relationship, causing irritations that could be avoided with this strategy of having a bit of time alone to relax.

Many people do not **know how to relate openly with others in the family.** As a result they think that the other person knows when they are sad, that they have not slept well, that they need love, or that they are profoundly hurt by something another person has said or done. They think, "If they loved me, they would know how I feel." However, truthfully, the person probably has given very vague messages of how they feel, and others may be totally in the dark as to these feelings.

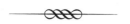

Our fatigue can rob us of our desire for relationship.

The reason for such vague messages of our true identity or our feelings is the fear that the person who knows more about you might reject or make fun of you, or even the specter of possible control or manipulation. A classic example of this is the wife who prepares a special meal, dresses attractively and plans for a romantic evening with her husband and he does not take notice of her special efforts. She is afraid to tell him, "I need you," because she is afraid of a possible rejection. However, this was the true message that she had wanted to relay to him with this special evening.

How many mothers feel profoundly hurt by the lack of attention by their children! They buy them gifts, do special things for them, but they are not capable of telling them how much they love them, how much they need them, how they want to help them and be a part of their growth and development.

In many occasions mothers are quarreling, fussing and complaining about their situation, when what they really want to say is, "Look at me," "Take me into consideration," "I love you," but they are afraid to put these feelings into words. As a result many begin to live a role of the suffering and rejected mother that they have seen in their own family, an action that leads to the breaking off of relationships and alienation within the family itself.

How wonderful it would be to become truly transparent and authentic and truthfully share who we are without fear of rejection. It will not always be easy to do so, but if we are going to achieve being a relational change agent we must make the effort.

Another barrier to communication is **silence.** Many times this is seen in the emotional withdrawal of a person when they neither communicate with nor relate to another person. They come home and retreat to the television, a book, the newspaper, a meal, a hobby, a sports activity, or work. Emotionally the person is like a phantom, a person totally detached from themselves and others.

Everyone needs their privacy and when it is managed adequately and protected for all members of the family, it helps to promote relationship, but healthy privacy and an emotional barrier that a person constructs around him/herself are two completely different situations. Emotional retreat is seen in many homes: the person is present, there is conversation, but they are not actively engaged. It is like relating to a dead person! The person hides behind the mask of friendliness, of kindness, of courtesy, of being helpful, but is not involved in relationships of the family.

It is easy to lose interest in communication and relationships when we have nothing in common with the other person. We live and relate in two different worlds. This can happen if one spouse or child becomes totally involved in their work, their study, their recreation, or some other interest. This happens frequently in marriages where one spouse develops in his/her professional or social life, while the other spouse remains bogged down or stuck in a previous level. There is no communication because they no longer have interests in common. Silence seems to reign in the home, and only the most perfunctory conversation is heard. This problem seems to be seen more frequently in today's economic setting. If both spouses are working outside of the home, frequently their lives develop more in the professional or work world in which they live, and there is little time left to relate meaningfully with the other. This can also happen when the wife is a homemaker and her world and that of her husband are so very different. Many times, perhaps without their realizing it, the relationship that had been so meaningful has become non-existent. In such a setting the whole family is affected, but especially the wife whose basic psychological self finds its meaning in affiliation and attachment.

Another form of retreat from significant relationships is **passive aggression.** Usually this is seen when a person is angry with someone, a member of the family, of someone at the workplace or school. The frustration or annoyance is not expressed openly, but rather in indirect ways. For example, doing things that annoy the person with whom he/she is angry. Many times this is done unconsciously. The person does not want to admit his/her true feelings. They deny their anger, and thus their action is unconscious. This action confuses the family, destroys relationships, and causes a sense of constant uneasiness. The person who is affected by this situation is confused and disoriented. Since they can't explain what has happened their reactions can become defensive and thus the situation deteriorates even more.

This is seen frequently among Christians who find themselves in these situations, because they do not know how to handle their anger. They believe anger is a sign of weakness for a Christian, and they tend to deny or censor its presence and attempt to eliminate it in their relationships, rather than finding healthy ways of expressing it. The logical consequence opens the way for such unconscious reactions as passive aggression.

All these barriers must be recognized for what they are by the Christian woman and her family. Each of us must determine to begin to eliminate them one by one. A good plan for beginning to resolve this situation is to confront it, name it for what it is, and question how this has become a barrier to healthy family relationships. In responding to this question you can then analyze how to eliminate it in order to improve relationships in the family. Remember that the barrier was not constructed in a day, thus it will take time, patience and constancy to lessen its power and finally eliminate it.

The barrier of **lack of time** requires a serious analysis of how you are using your time together. It should be coupled with a plan to organize your time so that you may include more quality time with your family. Of course there will be decisions that you and the members of your family will have to make. Many times you must choose among several things that you would like to do. Other times you will need to sacrifice some of the things that you have always done together because interests and needs have become more varied. Good organization of your time is a healthy tool to promote good and lasting relationships. However, it should never be a straight jacket to enact a rigid control on the family. A certain degree of spontaneity and flexibility in your schedule would be like a balm to the relationships in the family.

The problem of **fatigue** will be partially resolved as you work toward a better scheduling of your time. One of the most important steps for overcoming fatigue is a good night's sleep. This should be a habit, and not an exception to the rule. In addition a medical examination to ascertain any problems that might cause fatigue is essential. A good healthy diet and daily exercise are two of the most important aspects of a healthy lifestyle and the elimination of fatigue.

Not knowing **how to relate openly with others in the family** is a challenge for many as they struggle with their self-concept. At times this is based on a lack of self-esteem or self-knowledge. A careful reaching out to the person helping them understand themselves better is a good first step. Sometimes the person has built up resentment, or has learned to use deceit in his/her relationships. A loving mother can many times help a child bring these attitudes into the open through active and loving listening. To be able to communicate openly in the family is a blessed gift that family members can give to each other. It is a barrier that must be eliminated.

The problem of **silence** requires a change of conduct on the part of the person. You can be the key person to promote openness so that this person will begin to express him/herself more. Ask the person their opinion about different things, and listen carefully to the response, giving your complete attention so that they will know that you are listening, and that his/her opinion is important.

When silence is an indication of emotional retreat, try to get the person to open up to you, helping him/her to recognize that he/she is a person with feelings and ideas that should be expressed. Empathic attention to this person can help him/her to understand him/herself better and be more open to the family and others.

When silence is a sign of **passive aggression**, it is necessary to find its cause and then to help bring it out in the open and take the necessary steps to resolve it. Many times this kind of aggression is the result of rancor or grudges held and cultivated for a long time. It is traumatic to face them openly, but it is necessary if a healthy relationship is to survive. Facing them openly, but lovingly is the first step toward the elimination. Be aware of defensive attitudes that can enter into this process. They, too, must be eliminated as you proceed toward improved communication. Try to be open to any feeling that is expressed, and to search for understanding, mutual forgiveness, and the construction and development of healthier family and personal relationships.

The Christian family seeks daily to have a better relationship one with another. Eliminating barriers that exist will help you to make progress toward that goal.

Building bridges

It is true that no one is an island, separated from everyone else. However, many times we feel that we are an island, totally alone, even though we may be in the midst of a group of people or in our family. We need some means of relating to others, of reaching them and becoming a part of their actions. Bridges that make a difference and lead to a more positive relationship cannot be established only as a result of the functions or roles each person has in the family. Bridges must be developed in the area of our affections and our sentiments, and with the desire of establishing true relationships.

There are many reasons why we find ourselves distanced from other members of the family. Each one of us is distinct from everyone else, in our ideas, our sentiments, our way of resolving problems. In a family there are at least two generations, each with its own social and cultural orientation. Children and youth were born in the Technological Era. Their perspectives are very distinct from those of their parents, and a great deal more than that of their grandparents who were born into the Industrial Age. Each generation sees things differently, each uses a different vocabulary, each has values that are different from the others. Each generation even has a sense of humor that is different from the others! In many ways each group is an "isolated island," each in his/her own little world. It is necessary to build relational bridges of connection between these distinct groups.

The first bridge is **Unconditional Love.** In Colossians 3:14, Paul tells us that love is what "binds everything together in perfect harmony" and we can add that it is the perfect relational bridge. Love should not be conditional; rather it should be unconditional, a continual relational attitude, whatever may happen. This type of love does not demand a certain behavior before it is given to the other person. It is not based on exchange or barter, but it is a gift to the other person.

The Bible speaks of unconditional love. The people of Israel had a unique relationship with God because He had chosen them to be His special people.

> "For you are a people holy to the Lord, your God; the
> Lord your God has chosen you out of all the peoples on
> earth to be His people, His treasured possession....It was
> because the Lord loved you and kept the oath that He had
> sworn to your ancestors, that the Lord has brought you out
> with a mighty hand and redeemed you from the house of
> slavery, from the hand of Pharaoh king of Egypt"
> (Deuteronomy 7:6, 8).

Also we are told that "God proves His love for us in that while we still were sinners, Christ died for us" (Romans 5:8). Unconditional love is a relational bridge *par excellence.*

Love is not a passing emotion. Love is real and has to express itself in real ways.

Love cannot be repaid by a certain behavior or by doing something that pleases us or others. Love is a constant and unconditional acceptance of the person. In our excessively competitive world our children (or their parents!) can begin to believe that the family loves them only when they achieve something that gives the other person pleasure: a good grade in school, something the person does well, or a special honor that is highly prized by society. We must make it very clear to our children the difference between success and the pressure for recognition and that of love. Our understanding of these two positions is essential to the building of relational bridges.

There are two important facets in this bridge of love; one is tolerance and flexibility and the other is the ability to forgive.

For me, there is no greater picture of these two facets of paternal/maternal love than that of the parable of "The Prodigal Son." It has been said, however, that the real name of this parable should be "The Loving Father," because in it you can see the love of the father in spite of having been rejected and alienated by his son. The father listens to the demands of his younger son, and in a society where the son had no inheritance rights, the father was flexible, even though he knew that his son might waste the money he gave him. However, after experiencing the "joys" and the most crushing desolations of the city the son "came to his senses," and remembered his home and his family. This event teaches us a great truth about family life. Only those who "come to their senses" and remember their family are those who have had a family experience, an integral formation in that home. "Father, I have sinned against heaven and before you. I am no longer worthy to be called your son." The flexibility the father had shown in the past now allowed this son to "come to his senses." And the flexibility of the father permits him to say very wisely, "'…let us eat and celebrate for this son of mine was dead, and is alive again; he was lost and is found.' And they began to celebrate" (Luke 15:11-32).

The second bridge is that of **affirmation.** Many times family relationships are strained because there is never a true affirmation of the person. Affirmation is to name and affirm the positive qualities of the person. This is one of the greatest needs in our families. A great deal of criticism exists in the family, to the extent that some members think that that is the only way of relating one to another. Although honest criticism is necessary, many people take it to an extreme believing that in this way their *authority and position* are protected, and so they criticize others as each occasion arises. We should be very concerned if this is the only form of relationship in our families. Kind, thoughtful and truthful affirmation is essential to the construction of bridges that will bring the family into a more meaningful relationship.

Another destructive attitude which can destroy relationships is indifference, when it doesn't matter what the person may or may not do, the relationship is always the same, one of apathy. The person is treated with indifference. This attitude diminishes the value the person places on him/herself because he/she is treated as a "thing" and not as a person of value. Treating another with indifference not only separates individuals one from another, but also causes serious damage to their personalities. We were created for relationship and without it we become less that what God has planned for us to be.

We must be careful and not think that adulation or bragging are forms of affirming a person. Instead of being affirmations, they are alienating because the person who receives this adulation knows that it is undeserved and thus begins to doubt him/herself and the value of the relationship. They begin to ask themselves what is it that the person wants, what is he/she is trying to achieve, what will be the outcome of this type of relationship. As a result the distancing between the two grows with giant steps and the alienation becomes firmly entrenched.

On the other hand, a clear sign of emotional insecurity is that of a person who enjoys adulation and actually requires it for his/her personal functioning. The Christian mother, as a relational change agent, must be very careful to observe and redirect such procedures as she promotes healthy and long-lasting relationships among the members of her family.

Again, sincere affirmation is a relational bridge of great value. Such affirmation is to demonstrate the confidence that a person has in another person. It shows the faith that one has in the other, and in his/her ability. Sincere affirmation recognizes not only present qualities and actions of the person, but underscores the confidence and expectation of what he/she is capable of doing in the future. There is something that can be admired and affirmed in each person. As a relational change agent, use this position to affirm the members of your family.

Jesus gives us a wonderful example of the importance of affirming others to help them make better decisions for their lives. We see it in His relationship with Zacchaeus, with Matthew, the woman caught in adultery and other such persons. In each case He communicated to the person his/her value and their capacity to have a relationship with the Heavenly Father and to do more with their lives than they were presently doing.

Following in the footsteps of his Lord and Master, Barnabas, the Son of Consolation, was the person who affirmed the new believer Saul of Tarsus when everyone else doubted him. What would have happened to the missionary Paul if he had not had a Barnabas at such an important moment of his life? Surely the history of the world would have been different.

Many times the person most needy of affirmation is the one who is least apt to receive it. These persons can hide their need behind a guise of indifference, of a desire to "be friends with everyone," of either active or passive aggression, or of the chronic pain resulting from daily rejection which colors every moment of every day. We must be very careful to not show any difference among the members of our family, but rather to affirm each one for what he/she is, and for what they can become. Affirmation is a necessary and effective bridge that can be used by the relational change agent.

Another important bridge is that of **availability.** We must be available to our families, both in moments of sadness and pain as well as those of joy and pleasure. A mother does not have "office hours" to relate to her family. She must be available at any moment. This does not mean that she should take on the role of being a martyr, constantly complaining, "I don't have a free moment; never any time for myself." Mothers need others to be available to them also. She needs to feel that others are building bridges of relationship with her because she is valued in their eyes. However, she is the key person that can give this general tone and practice to her family. In his book, *The Wounded Healer,* Henri Nouwen[28] speaks of this same bridge as *"hospitality."* We must be hospitable with ourselves and with others, being ready to promote the emotional health that everyone needs. Hospitality is more than inviting someone into your home for a meal, or a child for a special outing. Hospitality can become a motivating part of relationship as we open our hearts one to another, as we make ourselves available one to the other.

Communicate clearly with your family that you are available to them at all times. Strengthen your words with actions and attitudes that will make the relationship even more meaningful.

Unconditional love, affirmation and availability are three essential bridges to build a healthier and more significant relationship with your family. As a mother and relational change agent you must dedicate yourself to both building these bridges and maintaining them in ways that will assure their long-term effectiveness.

Celebrating the relationship

Every family should celebrate the relationship that they have one with another. It is a great gift of God! It is the result of His love for each person, a love that stimulates our own love for Him and for others. To achieve a healthy relationship that will be more meaningful each day is of great importance for the family and for each of its members. This relationship should be recognized, appreciated and cultivated. One good way of doing so is to celebrate it!

It seems that our world has lost the true sense of what it means to truly celebrate something, but we must learn how to do so again. To celebrate is to remember, it is to emphasize something that is very important for the person, it is to be thankful, it is to recognize that life has its wonderful moments that need to be affirmed and celebrated. To celebrate is to join hands and thank God and the other person for what they mean to us. To celebrate is to be joyful for what has occurred in your life and in that of your family members and to affirm your belief in the good things that will happen in the future. To celebrate with your family is to believe in the family and all it means as a very special relationship.

Have a party, maybe a special meal, with flowers and candles on the table, thankfulness on your lips and contentment on your faces, love in your hearts and words of joy and gratitude on your lips, expressing to each other your true sentiments about the family relationship. A special celebration for a special family!

As a mother you can be a relational change agent in your family, promoting communication, eliminating barriers, building bridges, and celebrating the relationship you have achieved. No responsibility is more important, and no task you undertake more significant for the members of your family.

Activities for reflection and learning

1. Take the three bridges of relationship presented in this chapter: love, affirmation and availability and grade yourself as a relational change agent in your family. List at least one way in which you can use these three relational bridges with each member of your family. As you complete this activity, list how your actions were received and their results. Note how calling attention to each of these bridges has helped your relationships. This is an activity that would be beneficial to keep doing continuously.

2. Do your own Johari Window, analyzing each pane or quadrant as to where you are at this present moment in your life. What are the sizes of the different areas? What is the size of the "Open" pane? Should it be larger? If so, note how you would like to change it within a month, and what you would need to do to achieve this change.

3. Plan a party to celebrate the relationship that your family is achieving. Ask other members of the family to take part in the planning so that the whole family is involved in this important celebration. Perhaps you can have a serious moment in the celebration and ask for "testimonies" of how family relationships have improved, and ideas about how this can be continued.

4. Study Luke 15:11-32 to observe the interpersonal relationships seen of each person in the parable. Describe the way in which the father relates to each of his sons. How would you describe this father? What are the characteristics that enable him to relate to each of his sons differently as seen in this parable? How do you think that you would have helped the younger son? The older son? What would you have said to the younger son when he asked for his part of the inheritance?

Questions to answer alone or in a group:

• What does the word "relationship" signify for you?

• What does it mean to you that you are an "agent of relational change" for your own family?

- Who is the first person that you remember who really "understood" you and related well to you? What was he/she like? What effect did it have on you?

- Name three barriers to communication and relationship in your family. What can you do to eliminate them? Will you make plans to do so? How?

10. As a Minister Called by God

> *"Let the same mind be in you that was in Christ Jesus,*
> *who....emptied Himself, taking the form of a slave,*
> *being born in human likeness." Philippians 2:5, 7*
> *"Like good stewards of the manifold grace of God,*
> *serve one another with whatever gift each of*
> *you has received." 1 Peter 4:10*

One of the most important aspects of the church of Jesus Christ is that of the ministry of all believers. However, this basic concept has not been put fully into practice in many areas of our world. Ministry has been recognized as the responsibility of the pastor, known as "the minister." In the last thirty years, and especially in the last decade the church has been questioning this position and asking, "What is ministry?" and "Who is a minister?" This is occurring not only among evangelical and Protestant churches, but also in Catholic churches around the world.

With this renovation of interest in the ministry of the believer and of "the priesthood of every believer" as taught in the Bible, we need to have a clear idea of these concepts of ministry and the theology necessary to develop them. In addition we need to understand more clearly our identity as the "People of God," and as a person called to ministry.

As Baptists, Evangelicals or Protestants, we are in the line of the Reformation in which believers were called to return to the biblical teaching of the "priesthood of every believer" and of the importance of ministry for each person who is a follower of Christ. However, in spite of that fact that these concepts form such an important part of our religious heritage, we have not put them into practice. Many believe that the reason the modern church has failed in taking Christ's message of salvation to all the world is that we have not believed the truth that *every* believer is called to ministry. As a result we have deprived the world not only of the saving action of our Lord, but also of the social and ethical changes which the Gospel produces, establishing a better and more just society.

We are the "Laos," the "People of God." We have been called into a covenant with our Lord, and we have been sent as ministers in His name. In this chapter we will explore different aspects of ministry the Lord expects us to develop.

The meaning of Christian ministry

Christian ministry is a continuation of the work of Christ, done by the body of Christ, which is His church. It is a specific call that goes beyond the call to become a disciple of Christ, or our call to vocation, profession, or work. Colossians 3:17 helps us understand this call to ministry: "And, whatsoever you do, in word or deed, do everything in the name of the Lord Jesus, giving thanks to God the Father through Him." Our life is in ministry, a ministry to which God has called us. We are to be Christ's representatives, His ministers, His presence as we live our daily lives.

This ministry has been developed inside and outside the church as an institution, both in the church as an organization with its programs and activities, and outside of the church building itself in ministries and services. In addition, there is a ministry in the world, in secular life, in whatever profession or work the person may have. In each of these situations an act of ministry can take the love, the presence and the challenge of Christ into that setting. There Christians can console, teach, encourage, heal, and relate with those in need, with friends, with colleagues and others, giving testimony of the authenticity of their faith not only through their actions but through the way they think, relate and live their daily lives. The believer is called to ministry in whatever may be her setting: home, school, workplace, recreational activity. In each of these she is called to be a faithful witness and to extend the Reign of God in all the world. It is Christ who has given us an example of ministry and has called us to follow Him through our lives dedicated to doing His will.

In the New Testament, we find three basic truths of the concept of the ministry of the Laos, of the People of God.

1. **All are called.** "I therefore, the prisoner in the Lord, beg you to lead a life worthy of the calling to which you have been called." Ephesians 4:1

2. **All are gifted.** "But each of us was given grace according to the measure of Christ's gift." Ephesians 4:7

3. **All are sent to minister.** "Like good stewards of the manifold grace of God, serve one another with whatever gift each of you has received." 1 Peter 4:10

These passages together with the three great passages about spiritual gifts found in 1 Corinthians 12:4-13, Romans 12:4-8, and Ephesians 4:1-16 form a strong background for the ministry of each follower of Christ.

It is very significant for us that these passages that speak of the spiritual gifts do not emphasize the importance of the gift itself, but the need for each member of the body of Christ to work together using their spiritual gifts in the total work of the body. The interdependence among all parts of the body is emphasized as well as the mutual love that is to be the basic relationship of the whole body.

The Bible teaches that each person of the *Laos,* the people of God, is to participate in the Reign of God constantly. Since the King of Kings lives in us through His Holy Spirit, we are members of His kingdom and must serve Him as He has taught us. In order that we may fulfill the special ministry that He has given to each of us as believers, He has gifted us with His Holy Spirit. Dwelling in us, He is the source of power for our specific ministries. He leads us, guides us, and helps us remember the teachings of Christ. He encourages us, strengthens us, and helps us follow the leading of Christ. As we follow His guidance and are sustained by His support, our ministry is secure and will bring blessing to others and glory to our Lord.

The ministry of women

The ministry of the *Laos,* all the people of God, is for women as well as for men. In the Kingdom of God ministry is not accomplished through an agent or proxy. Each person is called to ministry and to a total commitment to that ministry. In addition, every Christian woman must find her identity in the people of God, an identity that will help lead her into the ministry to which God has called her. The emphasis given already in this book to understanding our identity as Christian women will be of great value as we seek to know our identity in the church and in God's call to ministry.

The Bible teaches that every person who has accepted Christ as his/ her Savior and Lord is accepted without discrimination as members of His kingdom.

"...for in Christ Jesus you are all children of God through

faith. As many of you as were baptized into Christ have
clothed yourselves with Christ. There is no longer Jew or
Greek, there is no longer slave or free, there is no longer
male and female; for all of you are one in Christ. And if
you belong to Christ, then you are Abraham's offspring,
heirs according to the promise." Galatians 3:26b-28

This "Magna Carta" of the faith gives us as women hope and a sense of
purpose. When there is discrimination in the church and women "are kept in
their place," we recognize that the larger vision of freedom as taught by Christ
(see John 8:31-32, 36) and Paul are still ideals and truth that we continue to
press toward, knowing that eventually they will become a part of the guidelines
of the church. But when they are missing, the body of Christ suffers and the
vision and the realization of the Day of Pentecost is lost in the face of legalistic
positioning (see Acts 2:14-41).

The Bible has many examples of ministries of women, some which we
have considered in previous chapters. Christ brought women to a new era, an
era of acceptance as a person of value. Their lives took on meaning that they
had not had before. They responded by giving their lives in loving service to
their Lord. It is interesting that the prophet Joel centuries earlier had spoken of
the day in which the Spirit of God would act in surprising and marvelous ways.

"Then afterward I will pour out My Spirit on all flesh;
your sons and your daughters shall prophesy,
your old men shall dream dreams
and your young men shall see visions.
Even on the male and female slaves,
in those days, I will pour out My Spirit." Joel 2:28,29

This prophecy was fulfilled on the great day of Pentecost when men and
women received the Spirit of God and entered into ministry from that very
moment. It was an effective ministry of sharing the Gospel that led to the
conversion of three thousand people. From the beginning of the church we
see women, as well as men, being equipped by God to carry on His ministry
in the world.

Should there be a different theological base for the call of women to ministry
that is distinct from that of men? Personally I do not think such a different
theological base exists, nor should it exist. In Christ there are no differences.
The theological base for the call of women to ministry is found in her having
been accepted as a member of the body of Christ. She is a co-disciple, a person
made in God's image, saved by faith in Christ, temple of the Holy Spirit, and

heir of the blessings of God for those who have entered into the New Covenant with Him.

In spite of this truth many women are not responding to the call of God to ministry. Perhaps their reticence comes from the idea that "ministry is for the minister," and women are excluded. Perhaps it is as a result of their ignorance of the freedom that they have in Christ, or their fear of entering into such a demanding ministry where there are many who would oppose such a possibility, even those in their own church family. All have ears, but many do not hear. As a result one of the most important tasks for the church is to help women hear the voice of the Lord calling them into ministry. Everyone, both women and men, must learn to become sensitive to the voice of God; to hear His call. When women hear the voice of God, and accept His call, clearly they "find their voice" and the world is blessed.

Both Christian women as well as the church to which she belongs must work together so that there will be more possibilities for women's ministry. The church must create a climate for the ministry of women by its teaching and its attitudes. It must offer training for those whom God has called. Women must be ready to grow as Christians and be continuously open and sensitive to God's call. They must seek training in order to serve their Lord in the best way. They must be authentic in their witness and in fulfilling the ministry to which God has called them.

Yes, there are more and more possibilities of ministry for women today, and many are already enjoying their service in the Kingdom. Women have served the Lord in many ways throughout the Christian era. When we read the history of the church we find that outstanding women servants of the Lord have been on the frontline of ministry both in the local church and in carrying the Gospel to foreign lands and peoples. In many countries throughout the world today women have been among the first converts, have shared the Good News with their family and neighbors in effective ways and have built the church into a strong witness in their communities. "Without the women" and their ministry, the church would not be where it is today. In many countries of the world women serve as missionaries, as Christian social workers, as church leaders, and as pastors in their churches. But this is not true in all countries and all churches. Because of her gender, women are restricted from many of the ministries of the church in many places in the world. As a result, we must continue our efforts until everyone, both men and women, are able to carry out the ministry to which God has called them.

The call to the pastoral ministry is often considered impossible or untenable for women. Many feel that it is not in "the nature" of women to fill the pastoral role and that Scripture dictates against it. However, as we have seen already women's special giftedness in affiliation, responsibility, connectedness, and relationships combine to give her special readiness for many of the demands of the pastorate. The Spirit of God continues to call women into pastoral service and the number of women pastors continues to grow in the world. Many have had to pay a very high price for their willingness to answer God's call to the pastoral ministry, but they have done so with determination to follow His leading and with grace in the face of opposition, and God has blessed their ministry.

The Scripture gives evidence of the effectiveness of women leaders since the early days of the church. I mention just one such example. In chapter 16 of Paul's letter to the Romans he sends greetings to a large number of his colleagues, people who have shared in ministry with him, and whom he acknowledges as co-ministers. Ten in this list are women! First there is Phoebe, the deacon (not deaconess) and the one to whom Paul has entrusted this important letter. Some say the word translated "deacon" here in other passages when speaking of a man is translated "minister." Whether or not this differentiation is intentional or a common gender bias, Phoebe was an important woman leader dedicated to the ministry of Christ and a trusted co-laborer with Paul. She had worked to benefit many in the church and was to be welcomed "in the Lord as is fitting for the saints" and helped "in whatever she may require" (Romans 16:2). In addition Junia is listed as "prominent among the apostles!" A woman apostle! There is Prisca (Pricilla), mentioned frequently by Paul as a gifted co-laborer, even mentioned first when listed with her husband, showing special respect and honor for her. The other women are Mary, Tryphaena, Tryphosa, Persis, Julia, and the sister of Nereus. It seems that in this important letter Paul had no trouble of recognizing women who served their Lord in ministry as did the men listed.

Early church women inspire us to serve Christ.

Other Scriptures give more problematic views of women, reflecting the culture of the day and the constant struggle between exercising the freedom that Christ had given and the restraints needed to ensure the continued existence of the church. Paul and other leaders recognized that they must not deviate too much from the cultural parameters of society, especially when

Christians were so few in number. The survival of the church depended on their circumspect behavior. We see this in the statement in 1 Peter, "Conduct yourselves honorably among the Gentiles, so that, though they malign you as evildoers, they may see your honorable deeds and glorify God when He comes to judge" (1 Peter 2:12).

There is not just one message about women in the New Testament. Rather we find Scriptures that give mixed positions on women. Some follow a strict patriarchal view, others speak of a partnership between men and women, and others return to a more limited patriarchal view. And so, again, we must be careful in our interpretation, remembering that the isolation of a text or taking it out of context can produce a mis-interpretation and can be harmful not only to women, but to the cause of Christ in the world. Good texts to remember as you listen to the voice of God for leadership as to how you will serve Him are John 8:31-32, 36, Galatians 3:28, and Acts 1:8.

Discerning God's will for my ministry

Can a woman be called, gifted and sent to ministry? Of course she can! The Lord involved women in His ministry. We see them in ministry in the pages of the Bible and in the pages of church history. From the beginning of the Christian era women have had many positions of ministry and they have developed that ministry in outstanding ways. We need to remember that many of our predecessors in Baptist life have been women who have had a ministry that they fulfilled to the glory of God. These women were preachers, biblical scholars, social workers, Christian Education specialists, missionaries and other varied forms of ministry. Many times they were pioneers in their ministries and the Kingdom of God was blessed with their service.

In the extension of the message of salvation in Latin America there would have been no Baptist work in many areas had it not been for committed and courageous women who were fulfilling the ministry that the Lord had given them throughout the length and breadth of the continent. I believe that many times these women did not realize that they were carrying out such an important ministry. For them, it was that they were doing their joyful duty as a follower of Christ to share the Gospel with others. They, like Peter and John, could have said, "Whether it is right in God's sight to listen to you rather than to God, you must judge; for we cannot keep from speaking about what we have seen and heard" (Acts 4:19-20). It was not for acclaim or to be "trail-blazers" that these women carried out their ministry but as committed followers of the Lord they were willing to sacrifice all they were in order to follow their Lord's leading in making His name known. Certainly this has been true in other parts of the world where women have had, and continue to have, major roles in proclaiming the Good News of Christ in a world that is ever more needy of its message.

While women "served" in many ways in expanding the work of the church in the past, times have changed. Today there is a need to talk about ministry. As Christian women called by God into ministry we must accentuate our calling, our giftedness and our preparation to serve the Lord. We must affirm our ministry and develop it with dedication as faithful servants of our Lord.

The following basic elements are essential for us to know the ministry to which the Lord is calling us.

First, I must **feel my calling.** In order to have a complete sense of my ministry, I must know that God can call me. I must know myself, believe in my value as a person, and be willing to listen to the voice of God. In the final chapter of the Gospel of John a fascinating and revealing conversation between Christ and Peter gives us a better understanding of how God calls a person to ministry, and recalls them when they are discouraged and ready to quit. In this case Peter was very depressed and isolated. He had left the ministry that Christ had given him because he was so ashamed of having denied his Lord. His shame had immobilized him and he decided to return to his fishing. In this chapter Christ reinforces that ministry with a new calling, one that is very personal, very specific, and "made to order" for this very special and capable disciple, but in this moment incapacitated by his guilt. What a wonderful passage for us to be able to contemplate! This experience should be remembered by Christian women who have been rebuffed in the expression of the ministry to which God has called them. In our moments of heartbreak and discouragement, Christ comes to us to renew our calling and to emphasize the importance of our ministry and the relationships we have with His people and with those do not know Him as Lord.

I think this is one of the most fantastic chapters of the Bible. Christ is giving new life and purpose to Peter, giving him courage, a new mind-set, and a new understanding of his calling to ministry. And, what is the outcome? Peter should have been celebrating this renovation and affirmation in ministry, but perhaps still not believing that it can happen to him, he asks Christ, "Lord, what about him?" referring to John. Christ responds with the reprimand, "If I want him to remain alive until I return, what is that to you? <u>You</u> must follow Me" (John 21:22 NIV). Our Lord insists that we fulfill our own ministry, and that we do not compare it with that of others. We must be in relationship with God to hear and feel our calling and thus to be able to celebrate it. The ministry to which each of us has been called is our own personal ministry. It is not like that of another person. God has called each of us by our name, and as we respond to His call each of us enters into a new relationship with Him in order to fulfill that calling.

Peter learned this truth and on the day of Pentecost we see him bringing the message of Christ's salvation to the throngs who were there for the feast and some 3000 believed in the Lord. And this was just the beginning of a long and blessed ministry based, no doubt, not only on the years of training with Christ, but this renewal and affirmation of the relationship with his Lord and the calling he had experienced anew.

Secondly, I must **feel an affirmation of my calling.** God has called me to ministry and has gifted me for that ministry, but though it is a personal calling, it must be fulfilled in community. My church, the body of Christ to which I belong, must affirm my calling to ministry. They must perceive my giftedness and my calling, and should communicate that to me. This should never be done in a non-personal way, but in a true co-participation in the reality of the special plan that God has for my life. At the same time I need to have affirmations from those with whom I live, or work, or study that they see and recognize evidences of my ministry in my daily life.

The words, "Thank you," spoken by someone who has benefitted from our ministry signify a great deal in the affirmation of our ministry. The sincere recognition of the evidence of ministry that has been carried out is life-affirming and life-changing for the minister. Many times that affirmation will come following what we may consider a failure in ministry, or something that has not been done well. The support, the recognition of efforts made, the words of encouragement can all be the difference between continuing in ministry or giving up to failure and disappointment. God does not call us to minister in a vacuum, but rather in the body of Christ and from that body we must receive the blessing of affirmation of our calling and of our ministry.

In third place, **I must feel the challenge to prepare myself for ministry.** When God calls me to serve Him, I should want to prepare myself for this service. I should not be satisfied with the *status quo*, but rather want to learn more and cultivate the gift He has given me. Paul counsels Timothy, "Do not neglect the gift that is in you, which was given to your through prophecy with the laying on of hands by the council of elders" (1 Timothy 4:14). In Romans he indicates that the person who is gifted by God for ministry should know how to share that gift with others (Romans 12:1-8).

We must prepare ourselves and equip ourselves for the ministry to which God has called us. When we discover our gifts and our ministry, then the Holy Spirit will lead us to understand our need to prepare ourselves more fully for service. As the Holy Spirit works in us and as we follow His direction, we will become more equipped to follow God's leadership in ministry. Preparing for ministry may require seminary or Bible School training that will enable us to be better equipped for the ministry to which God has called us. Such training should be embraced and celebrated for it will make each of us a better servant of the Lord in the ministry to which He has called us.

In fourth place, I need to **feel my responsibility to be accountable for the way I use my gifts in ministry.** The Bible teaches that spiritual gifts have been given for the building up of the body of Christ. Since there is this specific goal, when I know my gift/s I must be responsible to the church to which I belong for my use of those gifts in ministry. I need to know that my church is going to help me and encourage me in my ministry, but at the same time I must commit to being accountable to them, as my church, for the way in which I use my gift/s in ministry. For example, if I, as a member of this body of Christ, have been given the gift of exhortation, of encouraging others, I should give testimony as to how I have used this gift and the blessings that have resulted from this ministry. A serious and committed use of this responsibility will multiply the effectiveness of each gifted person as a servant of Christ and will enhance their mutual task of carrying forth the work of our Lord.

When there is no sense of accountability the person is bereft of guidance and directions that can make their ministry more effective. Often unaware of mistakes that are made in the carrying out of ministry the person can become discouraged or get into serious difficulties. The use of mentors and support groups is an excellent way to help the gifted person be accountable in the way she uses her giftedness in ministry.

In the fifth place, I need to **feel my calling to continue enlarging my ministry.** The person who is called to ministry knows that life is a process, and so is our ministry. There is a need to recognize the importance of seeing growth in the area of ministry. Just as our lives go from one stage to another, so our ministries need to develop, to become more profound, to find new ways of expression. Our growth in ministry, as in our life experience, must be holistic and integral. It must penetrate the total person and advance as it opens new ways of service to our Lord and to others.

The Christian life should never be routine, but rather, it should be vibrant, dynamic, exciting and open to all the possibility of growth and of finding new meaning and ways of fulfillment. This does not necessarily mean more activity, but rather being more sensitive to ways of carrying on ministry and the impact it can have on the lives of others. It means working and carrying out ministry in a more holistic way, with more devotion and more integrity. It means that as we sincerely and whole-heartedly enter our ministries we will begin to do away with our prejudices and the stumbling blocks that limit the possibility of true ministry. As we are healed ourselves we will be able to bring healing and health to others. As we experience more joy in service we will be able to carry that joy to others as well.

These five points are vital for our development in personal ministry. It is not possible to develop all of them fully at the same time for they are part of the process of a lifetime of service. However, we must begin the process if we are to achieve our goal. Note that each step has begun with the verb "**to feel**." These words mean commitment, involvement, and total surrender. When I am able "**to feel**" each of these steps then I will know that I do have the ministry to which God has called me, that I am able to carry it forth, that I am responsible for doing so, and that I can do so in the best way to glorify God and bring blessing to others.

Examples for my ministry

Each of us needs to have some examples of ministry that can help us see more clearly our own role and our own life in ministry. Of course, the Lord Jesus Christ is our primary example, our example *par excellence* of ministry. But in addition, the Bible is full of examples that can inspire our own ways of "doing ministry." Also, many of our own contemporaries offer us examples of how the Spirit of God guides in specific situations, reinforcing our ministry and our daily lives.

One night I sat down and began to list biblical examples for my life and my ministry. In a short time I had more than twenty names. Of course, there are many more if we should make a more complete study of these biblical personalities. In the following pages we will limit ourselves to consider four of these examples from the Bible, giving each one a contemporary "partner" to further stimulate our thinking and our action in ministry. We will see images that I feel are very applicable for the woman who knows her need of relationship and her sense of responsibility for others, qualities that are essential to who she is as a woman and for the ministry to which she has been called.

1. Treating others with dignity and respect

I believe that the message of the Bible tells us repeatedly that *every person is worthy of respect, and of consideration.* Jesus gives us many examples of this characteristic for our ministry. When He came for John to baptize Him, John refused. It is as if he said, "I am not worthy even to unlace your sandals, much less baptize you." Jesus must have looked John in the eyes and touched His shoulder and said, "John, you are the instrument that God is using to begin My ministry. You are a person of great value; you are worthy to participate in My kingdom and in God's plan." And John no longer hesitated, but baptized Jesus. (Read Matthew 3:13-17.) I believe that John was a changed man through this experience of *affirmation* by Jesus, an experience that accompanied him to his untimely death.

The experience of the woman caught in adultery is an exceptional example to help us understand the significance of treating others with dignity – gifting or gracing them with dignity. Many writers have commented on the kindness and human consideration of Jesus in this very legalistic situation. In order not to cause her more shame and thus crush her further, He did not even look at her during the time that her accusers were present. After they had all left, Jesus stood up and, I imagine, looked her in the eyes and asked, "Where are your accusers? Has no one condemned you? Has no one thrown a stone at you?" Her reply came in a barely audible voice, "No one, Lord." And Jesus, continuing to look at her with eyes of compassion, says, "Neither do I condemn you. Go and sin no more. You are a person of value; make your life show that value." (Read John 8:1-11.) What wonderful examples of the love and compassion that Christ had for people of His day – and of ours!

Christian women can treat others with dignity by the way in which they relate to others, resisting the temptation of making a difference between people, showing favoritism to some and indifference to others. I heard about a pastor who said that the first task of his ministry was to treat others with dignity and to produce a sense of dignity among the members of his congregation, among those to whom God had called Him to minister. What a wonderfully blessed congregation! Christian women can also grace others by the way in which they relate to them: treating them with dignity, infusing in them a sense of worth and dignity by the way she greets and talks with them – calling them by name, looking them in their eyes, listening to them, treating them as a person of worth, as they are in the eyes of our Lord.

In Bogota, Colombia, there is a Christian woman who has felt the call of Christ to minister to prostitutes. One could say that this is too large a problem and one person would not change things very much among the thousands of women who ply this trade. However, this woman is called to this ministry and she works in the rehabilitation of twenty-five ex-prostitutes. She teaches them dressmaking and has a shop where they are employed and where their small children are taken care of and meals are provided for all of them. These women are treated as persons of value in a ministry that attempts to meet their needs in a comprehensive way. Through this ministry these women and their small children have a new lease on life, and for the first time in their lives they have been gifted with hope for a better future. They have been treated with dignity as persons created in God's image and valued in His sight.

I have had a similar experience in working with illiterates. As a person learns to read and write and begins to function better in society he/she begins to have a greater self-appreciation as a person, to feel his/her own personal worth and dignity. The key for this new life comes not only from the new skills that are being learned, but also from the personal and meaningful relationship and treatment between the two persons in a ministry that seeks to treat others with dignity and as persons of value.

2. Humanity that produces more humanity

Usually we do not speak of the humanity of God, but rather we speak of His divinity. However, I want to use this concept in this way here. John tells us that God "became flesh and lived among us" (John 1:14). He came to the world through His Son who lived among us, giving us an example of His desire to show what humanity could be, of how people could relate in more humane and caring ways one to another. In reality God has given us meaningful examples of this quality in the way He demonstrates His love for us, beginning in creation, making male and female alike in His image and likeness, and continuing through His intervention in the lives of so many whom we encounter in the

Bible and in everyday life. In treating us in these ways He stimulates in us a desire to appropriate these same qualities in our lives and in our relationship with others.

In interpreting the Parable of the Good Samaritan it has been suggested that Jesus told this parable to appeal to our humanity, to help us sympathize with the person who is wounded, the victim, and to respond to the sentiment of responsibility and caring for others within ourselves. When we do so we are not a part of the dehumanizing actions of those who "pass by on the other side." Rather we are among those who are "moved to pity," who draw near and do something for the wounded person (Luke 10:25-37). It is true that when we see the humanity shown by others, it is like a catalyst producing more humanity in us.

We should not forget that Jesus told this parable in order to emphasize the importance of being a good neighbor to another person. The good neighbor is exemplified in the Good Samaritan, a person who was typically rejected and alienated from Hebrew society. Surely he must have experienced this alienation personally in his many trips into Jewish territory, yet he did not let it determine who he was as a person, as one who cared for others. Here he is the one who treats the needy person, a Jew, in a loving and caring way, when those of the wounded man's own race, even religious leaders, treat him in a dehumanizing way, "passing by on the other side." Jesus gives us an eternal teaching in the example of the Good Samaritan as one who was moved with pity for an unknown person in need of care. He affirmed this response to another human being, when He said, "Go and do likewise." (Luke 10:37b). Treating another in a humanizing way produces a greater sense of humanity. Today all over the world there are reminders of the actions of this good and caring man in hospitals, clinics, ministries, and social services which bear the name of the "Good Samaritan".

Helen Barnette[29] in her book, *Your Child's Mind: Making the Most of Public Schools,* speaks of a moving experience that happened in her classroom, that I think shows this basic biblical emphasis in a marvelous way. Mrs. Barnette was a teacher in a public school in Louisville, Kentucky. She was a Christian who felt a divine call to the ministry of teaching. She always had a strong sense of her responsibility as a Christian which was seen in the way she treated her twelve and thirteen year old adolescent pupils with respect. Some of these students came from broken homes and had had a history of problems and they needed a teacher like Helen Barnette in their lives.

It was the day before Thanksgiving and Mrs. Barnette had told her pupils of the first class that since it would be the day before this important holiday, she was going to read them a story she knew they would like. But in the early hours that day she had received news of the death of a close friend, a Christian humorist. She was not sure if she could go to school because of her grief, but since it was the day before Thanksgiving she also knew that it would be difficult to find someone to take her place. And, so, she went to school.

When the pupils in her first class arrived she had them put their chairs in a circle to read them the story. She began telling them what it was to write something that showed humor, and that made her think of her friend who had died. When she began to read the story, which was written in the dialect of the South, she remembered how her friend used this dialect in many of his programs and suddenly she stopped reading and began to weep silently. Her students looked at her unbelievingly. One student who was seated by her side put her arm around her shoulder and patted her as a mother consoles her child. When Helen gained a bit of composure, she told them of the loss of her friend, and her students began to comfort her.

One said, "I bet it was that Grady Nutt. I heard it on the news this morning." "He was good. He spoke at our church." Another commented that he had seen him on television. "We all like him 'cause he made everybody laugh." Another commented about how he had visited her grandfather in the hospital. In this way these young people took part in the grief of Helen and comforted her. After a while, she told them, "My friend loved young people. I want you to know that I love you, too. You have helped me by being kind and letting me cry. I am so grateful that you are my first-period class; for I know that if I can just get through *this* period, I can get through the rest of the day. You are very special to me and I thank you."

Helen finished the class and her pupils left, but several times during the day these students came by her classroom to see if she was doing well, and if she had been able to have her classes. Later, one girl who had a truancy problem in the school, who lived in a foster home, and was unhappy in her first year at this school, came and put her arm around her shoulder and with a very special care and interest asked, "Are you all right? Are you making it through the day?"

This moving experience shows the ministry of empathy, of feeling what the other person is feeling, of being able to identify with another, of treating another human being in a humanizing way. As the result of the way she had treated her pupils before this day, in this moment of grief Helen Barnett could not only show her humanity, expressing her grief, but there was a feeling of mutual empathy between her and her pupils. All of them became more human as a result of sharing grief and feeling compassion for another person.

Wouldn't you like to have had Helen Barnette as a friend or as a teacher for your children or your grandchildren? You, too, can have a ministry of treating others in a humanizing way. As we show these more human characteristics, we enable others to be more human also. Jesus says, "Go, and do likewise."

3. Hospitality

The Bible says that we should be hospitable to others. "Be hospitable to one another without complaining. Like good stewards of the manifold grace of God, serve one another with whatever gift each of you has received" (1 Peter 4:9-10). In addition, hospitality is mentioned in the list of spiritual gifts found in Romans 12:13.

The Bible mentions the idea of hospitality time and time again. In the Old Testament there is the Shunammite couple who built an upper room for Elisha (2 Kings 4:8-10). Martha, the sister of Mary and Lazarus, opened her home to Jesus and His disciples on many occasions. In the early days of the church many families opened their homes to their fellow believers so that they might worship and pray together. The qualities necessary to be a pastor ("overseer" or a "bishop") included hospitality (1 Timothy 3:2 and Titus 1:8) and the writer to the Hebrews reminds readers, "Do not neglect to show hospitality to strangers, for by dong that some have entertained angels without knowing it" (Hebrews 13:2).

I want us to consider especially the example of Lydia, the hospitable woman in Philippi. She was already a woman who was seeking to know the true God; she and other women met together by the riverside to pray on the Sabbath. It was there that Paul and Silas found them. As she heard the words of Paul, the Lord opened her heart and following her baptism as a new believer in Christ she pled with Paul, "If you have judged me to be faithful to the Lord, come and stay at my home" (Acts 16:15). Her home became not only a "home away from home" for the missionaries, but the base of the evangelistic activities in Philippi and it is to Lydia's home following the night in prison, to which Paul and Silas return, "and when they had seen and encouraged the brothers and sisters there, they departed" (Acts 16:41b).

If we only had these verses in Acts to recognize the value of Lydia, perhaps she would not be such an example for the ministry of hospitality. However, when we compare the 16th chapter of Acts with the letter to the Philippians with all its expressions of joy, of love and of such a meaningful relationship between Paul and this church which continued to support him in his missionary activity, we can see the impact of the ministry of Lydia in the formation of this community. From its very beginning there was an open heart and an open home, and the Gospel took root and grew! This church became one of Paul's most consistent helpers. His meaningful words of gratitude and love are felt in these brief chapters. (See Philippians 1:3-5, 7, 8; 4:1.) He writes, "I rejoice in the Lord greatly that now at last you have revived your concern for me; indeed, you were concerned for me, but had no opportunity to show it.... You Philippians indeed know that in the early days of the gospel, when I left Macedonia, no church shared with me in the matter of giving and receiving, except you alone" (Philippians 4:10, 15). I believe that Lydia's ministry of hospitality was an important factor in the growth of the church. In addition, it was an example to other churches then, as it is today.

Hospitality is a spiritual gift that is foundational to ministry. It must be practiced in the home and outside the home, with consideration and attention to others. It is a gift that is seen especially in women who open their homes to others, who maintain relationships with others and participate in the life of persons who are far away from their families or need a family with whom they can relate.

I have a Christian friend in Cali who is truly a hospitable person. She knows how to receive people into her home. She is always ready with a cup of coffee and a cookie for the person who needs to talk with her. She also opens her home to people who need to spend a night or two. She opens her home to groups who come to make craft items, and others who come for Bible classes, cooking classes, or English classes. All are welcome. She uses her home in her ministry, and people come because they know that they are welcome and that they will be blessed.

Hospitality is more than opening your home to others; it is also opening your heart to those who need a friend, who need someone who wants to relate to them. The key to the ministry of hospitality is love for others, an unconditional love. One of the best ways to use your home in this ministry today is through home Bible studies where all are received with love, treated as persons of value and where life-changing relationships are formed. To visit a home such as this is to receive the blessing of a very special ministry.

4. Developing confidence

The Bible emphasizes the need of having confidence in God. When we know we can trust God, be confident of His presence and guidance, we can go about our lives knowing that He is with us. Jeremiah gives a picture of just such a life:

> "Blessed are those who trust in the Lord, whose trust
> is the Lord. They shall be like a tree planted by water,
> sending out its roots by the stream. It shall not fear
> when heat comes, and its leaves shall stay green; in the
> year of drought it is not anxious, and it does not cease to
> bear fruit." (Jeremiah 17:7,8)

Truly such confidence gives stability and hope to life.

On the last night of His life, Jesus wanted to strengthen the confidence of His disciples, assuring them time and time again of the faith and trust that each one of them could feel. "Do not let your hearts be troubled. Believe in God, believe also in me….I will not leave you orphaned, I am coming to you…. Take courage; I have conquered the world" (John 14:1, 18; 16:33). Jesus gives us courage and confidence for our daily life.

Women enter into a very important ministry when we follow the example of our Lord and instill confidence in our children, helping them to have a continual sense of confidence in themselves, in their world, in their relationship with God and their fellow human beings. Famous psychiatrist Erik Erikson[30] says that it is in the first stage of life when a child learns the basic trait of confidence or lack of confidence, according to the way in which they are treated by the mother or their primary caregivers. If the child can be confident in the words of the mother, of the way in which he/she is held and carried, in her presence, her touch, the constancy and truthfulness she shows, then this child will carry this confidence on through adolescence and adulthood. If, on the other hand, the child does not learn to have confidence in his/her mother, then he/she will be mistrusting, nervous, and suspicious of others. Life will be difficult, both for the person and for those he/she relates to. There is ample evidence of women's influence on their children and of the powerful ministry they have in their hands. "…let it be said here that the amount of trust derived from earliest infantile experience does not seem to depend on absolute quantities of good or demonstrations of love, but rather on the quality of the maternal relationship."[31] As we relate one to another, lives can be blessed. This is one of the most precious gifts that we can receive from another person.

Dorothy Söelle[32] tells of a little Jewish girl who sang, "I am beautiful, beautiful. My name is beautiful." This song expresses the confidence of this child in life. When a person has had a happy and full childhood, one that has provided a basic trust and confidence in life and in others, then they can live confidently and see their world as trustworthy and themselves as acceptable and important to others.

Women can be the key to the confidence and self-esteem that their children need throughout life. As we prepare our children for school with such illusion, one of the most important aspects of that preparation is to have instilled a sense of confidence and trust by the way we have related to them in their earliest years. Again, one of our most important ministries!

I know a woman whose daughter had some problems in school in one of her subjects. She was a normal child, intelligent, but perhaps lacked the discipline and attention that was needed to learn to write and read correctly. Her first grades were very low, and were accompanied with notes from the teacher that she must improve. The girl was ashamed, feeling that she couldn't learn. The mother began to work with her daughter. She found books and information on phonetics and, using games, helped the child to define and pronounce the syllables and then to join them so that she could read and write them correctly. Soon the child went to school with a great deal more confidence. They had been able to avoid the possibility of an embittered and ashamed child, stigmatized in her class. This, too, was the ministry of a mother who was giving confidence to her daughter who needed it.

I think the ministry among children who are abused and mistreated is one of the most important that women are doing all over the world. The sad reality of child abuse in its multiple forms causes the child to not trust anyone. However, through the unconditional love and care of a person who has entered into this ministry the child can be healed and can enter into a new life in which he/she can have confidence and trust in others.

There are women who have entered into this ministry, going to the homes or to institutions where these abused children live. As a result of their long-term commitment they are able with love, tact, constancy and understanding to instill a sense of confidence and trust in the child. Women have the unique possibility of this specific ministry with their own children, with the children of the church, with children of their community, and with those who have been abused. This is one of the ministries where positive and transforming changes can be seen. Physical, emotional and spiritual needs can be met. Lives can be changed! Lives can be saved!

Another form of this ministry is to work with women who have been abused, have suffered from addiction, or who because of these problems and poverty have not had opportunities to study and prepare themselves adequately to get employment. One of these ministries is called the Christian Women's Job Corps in which women in these conditions are offered a Christian setting where they can be mentored by a Christian woman, and through that relationship, Bible studies, job training, and other programs can improve their lifestyle, begin to have a sense of self-confidence and trust, can find employment and new meaning for themselves and their families. Truly a life-changing ministry! Be a woman who instills confidence and trust in others!

These four examples of ministry found in the Bible and in our contemporary world are resources and reinforcements for our ministry as women, but they are only the initial first step. There are many other examples in the Bible and in everyday life that call us to amplify our ministry, to find where and how we can be ministers for God in our homes, in our work, in the community, in the church and in the world. Look for additional examples that can serve as a stimulus for your creativity as the Holy Spirit leads you. As you see more possibilities of ministry you will be able to be able to follow God's leading in being the minister He would have you be.

Every Christian is called, gifted and sent into ministry. The ministries that God puts before us are as diverse as the opportunities of life. Their development will depend on how each person responds to God's voice and the opportunities around them.

I'm called! I'm gifted! I'm sent into ministry by God! I will be a good administrator of the gifts that God has given me. I will be a minister in Christ's name.

Activities for reflexion and learning

1. Describe a ministry that you have observed a woman doing in your church or in another church. What are her spiritual gifts? How does she use these gifts inside and outside the church building?

2. Do you know a woman who is in the pastoral ministry? What are the outstanding characteristics of her ministry? Are they different from those of male pastors? If so, in what way?

3. What are your spiritual gifts? How did you come to understand that you are gifted in this way? Has your church and have other people affirmed your gifts? How? How do you respond in accountability to your church for the way you use your gifts? Are you faithful in doing so?

4. Study Philippians 2:5-11 in order to receive from this great passage criteria that you can use in your own ministry and accountability.

5. Without opening your Bible make a list of persons found there who can be an example for your ministry. Afterwards, read one of the gospels looking for examples for your ministry. Compare the two lists. What are the characteristics of ministry that you find most frequently in the Bible? How can you put these into practice in your life as a minister and servant of the Lord?

6. Are there ministries that you could enter into with another person in which the distinct gifting of each would complement that of the other person? Make a plan for a shared or complementary ministry with this person.

7. Prepare a sermon, a class, a conference or a testimony that you could give in the church as one who is a minister of Jesus Christ. Choose scripture that will give a positive reflection of your call to ministry and how you are fulfilling that call.

Questions to answer alone or in a group:

*   Are there spiritual gifts that are more suitable for women? Name them. Explain your answer.

*   What does it mean to be a woman in ministry? What are the essential criteria for the development of ministry? Are these different for a woman than those of men? Why or why not?

*   What is your favorite biblical example to reinforce your concept of ministry?

    How can you use this example in your own ministry?

11. As a Developing and Maturing Christian

> *"But grow in the grace and knowledge of our Lord*
> *and Savior Jesus Christ." 2 Peter 3:18a*
> *"And may the Lord make you increase and abound in*
> *love for one another and for all....And may He so*
> *strengthen your hearts in holiness that you may be*
> *blameless before our God and Father at the coming of*
> *our Lord Jesus with all His saints."*
> *1 Thessalonians 3:12a, 13a*

Dorcas had died and the believers in Joppa were grief-stricken. What would they do without her – this woman who lived a life of selfless love for others? The disciples knew that Peter was nearby in the city of Lystra, and they had heard of the miracle he had preformed there in healing the paralyzed Aeneas, and so they sent two men to ask him to come to be with them: "Please, come to us without delay" (Acts 9:38b). What had the believers thought that Peter might do in this sad moment? Was it perhaps that he might be able to console them, since he had experienced grief in such a very intense way in the death of Christ and his denial of Him? Was it that he might stay with them during this time of their loss and tell them more about Jesus' life and teachings? Could it have been the hope that Peter might be able to bring her back to life so that she might continue her loving ministry among them? Why was Dorcas so special?

Dorcas was a believer who "...was devoted to good works and acts of charity" (Acts 9:36b). Her good works included the tunics and other clothing that she had made for the widows and for others in her community. However, there must have been other ways in which this woman related to the people of Joppa as she helped them. In the Bible alms or charitable giving were the monies given for the upkeep and the ministry of the Temple and the Levites who served there. So, Dorcas abounded in acts of kindness and care of those in need. She loved God and she was happy to be His co-laborer and to join others of this group of believers in the ministry to which He had called them.

I believe that if Dorcas was alive today and we could ask her to explain the theological basis for her ministry, she would use relational concepts as she would talk of the importance of relating to God and to others. It would be impossible to separate her faith from the way in which she related to those to whom she ministered. Indeed, it was the very heart of her ministry. When Dorcas gave one of the tunics she had made to a needy person, it wasn't just an automatic impersonal act of giving, it was a time of lovingly relating to this person. Dorcas was a relational person and she is an example for us.

In this chapter we will base our study on the concepts found in Relational Theology because I believe that this, more than any other theological approach, is most apt for our needs as women. We have seen that our way of thinking and our basic psychological orientation is relational, and so, Relational Theology has a special significance for us, opening opportunities for ministry and for understanding God's purposes for His creation not found in other approaches. It is a theology that can be understood as a lifestyle that tries to stimulate Christian growth and the vitality of the church through the relationship of Christians. It promotes openness, acceptance, responsibility and the systematic growth of personal faith. This theology is not exclusive, nor selective, nor does it grade believers according to the manifestation of their spiritual life. Rather it emphasizes the importance of the presence of God found in relationships, both with Him, and with others.

This concept is very stimulating to me as a woman. I believe that it offers a greater possibility for me to develop my personal theology in a logical, conscientious, functional and stimulating way. Who am I? I am a woman in relationship, a person to whom relationships are important. How can I best give expression to my Christian life? How can I grow with my Lord and my neighbor? The answer is in relationships. How can I continue my growth and my development as a Christian woman? The answer is in relationships that give meaning and satisfaction to my life. I challenge you to look for ways to relate with others in a more significant way. Analyze your relationships as part of the growth process in your Christian life. Are there relationships that have made such an important impact on your spiritual life that you know that as a result you have grown in maturity with your Lord? Are there relationships in ministry in which you have been able to mentor another person and see them begin to grow and make plans for a more promising future? In this chapter we are going to consider three areas of our lives, three concepts that are basic to Relational Theology: my life as a believer, my ministry and my lifestyle.

Growing in my life as a believer

Relational Theology emphasizes the importance of the relationships of the believer. Jesus gives us the example of the small group with the twelve disciples. There was interdependence and a creative relationship among them. We see this also in the early church with the small groups that met to eat together, to share in a life of prayer, in worship and service among the extended community.

When a Christian begins to live in a relational way there are special characteristics that begin to be normative in their lives. Relational theology helps us to be able to emphasize the importance of the following:

1. **Being a new creation**

   "So if anyone is in Christ, there is a new creation, everything old has passed away; see, everything has become new" (2 Corinthians 5:17). Following the new birth the believer now has different perspectives, new desires, and new attitudes that are the result of her affiliation, relationship and loyalty to Christ. There are new ways of seeing and experiencing. The moment of conversion is not the culmination of one's experience with Christ, but rather the moment of a new beginning in the way of discipleship and of becoming the person that Christ would have her be. The new Christian, this new creation, is to be growing constantly and pressing on toward the goal of knowing and becoming more like the Lord. The words of Paul become our own expression of commitment, "I press on to make it my own, because Christ Jesus has made me His own" (Philippians 3:12b).

   To be a new person in Christ is to "put off" the old ways of doing things and to "put on" new ways, new approaches to life, a new way of being. Again Paul says, "You were taught to put away your former way of life, your old self, corrupt and deluded by its lusts, and to be renewed in the spirit of your minds, and to clothe yourselves with the new self, created according to the likeness of God in true righteousness and holiness" (Ephesians 4:22-24). We join with God in this total change and become a new creation. As a result we are able to relate to Him and to others in new and affirming ways.

2. Openness to Life

"But if we walk in the light as He Himself is in the light, we have fellowship with one another, and the blood of Jesus His Son cleanses us from all sin" (1 John 1:7). To walk in the light is to leave the darkness and being seen as we truly are. The idea of walking here refers to our lifestyle, of how we live our lives daily. It is to be open to who you are and to who you can become. The Scripture says that two things happen when we are open to life as we walk in the light: (1) we have communion (*koinonia*) one with the other, and (2) the Lord is continually cleaning us from all sin. The idea of being open to life is that of transparency. When we are not sincere, or transparent, we are not walking in the light. We become afraid of the light, of being seen as we truly are and we seek the shadows to cover us. Our relationship with God and with others becomes superficial. We have too much to hide!

Walking in the light is to be open to the light of God. This light reveals our sins, but at the same time it enables us to receive cleansing from our sins. The light acknowledges the forgiveness of our sin, bringing not only healing but affirming the new relationship we have in Christ Jesus. Light is the symbol of the presence and the activity of God. With His light we can be open to life; we can live with transparency.

3. Having Freedom in Christ

"If you continue in My word, you are truly My disciples, and you will know the truth, and the truth will make you free" (John 8:32). This freedom signifies that we can develop our spiritual life without limitations and the control of other people. Nevertheless we must recognize that in many ways we are influenced, controlled, and limited by significant persons in our lives. In addition, we are controlled by our own personality and the way we develop into the person we are, as well as by the limitations placed on us by our environment, the church and the Christian community to which we belong. These limitations and controlling influences remind us time and time again that we must maintain our eyes upon our Lord and His example, as we face the challenges of our daily lives. His presence in our lives enables Him to remind us of the freedom that He has given us, and the way it can continue to bless us and make us a blessing to others.

Relational Theology teaches that we have freedom as a result of our relation with Christ and our dedication to Him. (See John 8:31-32, 36.) When we live in relationship with the Lord and with others, there is the possibility to grow in God's plan for our lives. Only in this way is there personal and relational freedom. Paul counsels us about the danger for our spiritual life, "For freedom Christ has set us free. Stand firm, therefore, and do not submit again to a yoke of slavery" (Galatians 5:1). In Christ we have a sense of security that reinforces the freedom He has brought us. This is one of the precious gifts of God which we must use for our growth and relationship with Him and with others. We must stand firm in our commitment to Christ and in the freedom He has given us!

4. Growing in Faith

"But speaking the truth in love we must grow up in every way into Him who is the head, into Christ" (Ephesians 4:15). One grows in Christ when we seek to follow Him constantly. The pilgrimage of our salvation is a pilgrimage toward wholeness. It includes growth in every aspect of our lives as we become co-laborers of our Lord and witnesses to others of His presence and leadership.

Relational Theology helps us understand that some people are content with what they have achieved in their spiritual life and thus become stagnated where they are. Others place impossible goals for themselves and continuously consider that they are a failure in their spiritual growth. Each of us should be asking ourselves: "What are my spiritual needs?" "How can I grow in my faith?" "Which are the areas of my life that need to be changed?" "Which require learning something new that will promote more spiritual growth?"

There are four basic relationships in this theological approach to our spiritual growth: (1) our relationship with God, (2) our relationship with ourselves, (3) our relationship with others who are important in our lives, and (4) our relationship with our world. In each of these relationships there are always areas that demand our attention and our willingness for growth. We need to ask ourselves, "What are the areas of our lives that are 'stuck'?" "What are the wounds and hurts I carry that need healing?" "Am I disoriented in some area of my life?" "Am I reaching my potential as a Christian?" In facing these questions we will find a starting place from which we can grow toward our potential, always reminding ourselves of the presence of Christ within us to strengthen and guide us.

Relational Theology is based on a personal experience of faith. Without this experience there will be no significance to our lives. With it, life can become a path toward the development and realization of the potentiality which God has for each one of us.

Growing in my ministry with others

The second concept for developing my faith has to do with my ministry with others, what I feel that God wants me to do as His beloved child. He has called me, gifted me and sent me to ministry in relationship with my world. What does that mean for me? Relational Theology helps us understand more completely the specific functions a Christian has in ministry. In continuation we will consider those functions that are basic and needed for growth in ministry in a relational way.

1. Help Others in their Christian Life

The concepts of communion, of *koinonia* and of relationships within the family of God are all foundational to the Christian life. Every Christian has a ministry of promoting and helping in the development of the Christian life of others. The concept of therapeutics is not only found in modern psychology, but it is basic to the Christian life. There are ways of bringing healing to medical needs, but there are also ways of bringing healing relationally and spiritually. We have already studied and affirmed this concept, especially in the marital relationship, but here we will emphasize five ways Christian women can promote healthy growth in the life of other followers of Jesus Christ. Incidentally in doing so, they, too, will receive the blessing of healing and growth.

- **Affirmation..** When Barnabas, the Son of Consolation, related to others, he knew how to affirm them in their personal and spiritual life. (See Acts 11:19-26). We can emulate his actions as we communicate to others that they are persons of great value, that they have positive qualities, that they are persons in whom you can see the presence of God. Relational Theology teaches that when a person believes that others see them as persons of value, they are able to remove their defensive posture because they no longer have to be constantly proving their worth in relationship to others. They can begin to affirm all that is good in their lives, and as a result they come to the point where they are willing to correct aspects of their lives that need change. Affirmation opens the way to growth in Christ.

- **Confession.** "Therefore confess your sin to one another" (James 5:16a). While we need to confess our sins to God, in many occasions both spiritual and emotional health depend on our disposition to confess our spiritual condition to another person. The person who is ministering to another person in this situation should be a helper who knows how to listen and to affirm the grace of God to pardon sin. They should be able to pray for the health and growth of the person who has confessed her sin. This is truly to be a therapeutic person, one who promotes health and development. Personally I do not believe that confession should be made in a session of the church, but in relationship with another person, or in a very small group of people who are committed to confidentiality and would never use these experiences to gossip about the person or to use them is some other destructive or controlling way.

We are all sinners; all of us need to confess and to receive pardon. God calls us to recognize and confess our sin, to repent for those sins we have committed, to receive His pardon and determine not to repeat these actions, but rather to walk in obedience to His teachings. What a great and liberating blessing to be able to follow His way and to help another to do so also.

- **Carrying the Burdens of Others.** "Bear one another's burdens, and in this way you will fulfill the law of Christ" (Galatians 6:2). By being compassionate and understanding we can help others bear their heavy burdens. To be understanding and affirming of another person who has a heavy burden to carry can give them new life, new hope to be able to bear their own burdens, hope that will enable them to better face their difficulties and be able to help others who may be in need. Without a doubt the person who has helped in this way will have new strength for bearing their own burdens also.

There are many burdens in life, and they touch every area of our lives. They can be in the losses we experience – a job, a home, a child, a parent, a spouse, a marriage, health, status and so many other ways. But there are the burdens of oppression, of injustices done by another or by the social environment in which we live. There are the burdens of illness, of chronic diseases that sap the essence of life from the person and their families, of debilitating accidents, of terminal illnesses, all of which cause additional physical, emotional and spiritual stress. There are the burdens of poverty, social status, and cultural requirements. As we enter into these situations and carry the burden of another we become a co-worker with Christ, fulfilling His law and sharing His grace! What a privilege!

One of the burdens women and children, especially girls, carry is the oppression they suffer in many parts of the world. The economic and social realities that force them into prostitution; the illnesses they sustain; the difficulties and lack of adequate care in childbirth that cause trauma or death; the lack of educational opportunities which might give them some freedom from the burden of poverty and oppression are all heavy burdens that we as women need to help oppressed women carry. We can do so as we personally help in some specific situation of need in our community and as we become advocates for women's and children's rights in all parts of the world. We can join hands with other Baptist women through the Baptist World Alliance Women's Department in efforts to make our world a better place for everyone, bringing positive change for a more just and equitable society, and a more promising future for women and girls in all parts of the world. In addition, we can join them and other groups in working toward the Millennium Development Goals which are focused on bringing about change by 2015 in eight specific areas of social ills around the world. These goals are focused on relieving and eliminating the heavy burdens that women carry in many parts of the world, burdens that we can lift and them help carry. (See Appendix A.)

- **Affirming Spiritual Gifts.** "We have gifts that differ according to the grace given to us…" (Romans 12:6). As we have emphasized in a previous chapter one of the responsibilities of the Christian community is to help one another discover, develop and use the spiritual gifts God has given each of us for our ministry in the church and in the world. We should be aware of the needs in our midst and try to see how the gifts of each person can be used to fulfill them. In the Christian community gifted people should be commissioned so that they might use their gifts in ways that would bring maximum blessing to others. Also, we should be careful to take time to affirm the ministry that is carried out by fellow Christians who are using their gifts and their calling to bring blessing to others and glory to God.

• **Prayer.** "Pray for one another so that you may be healed. The prayer of the righteous is powerful and effective" (James 5:16). One of the most important foundational aspects of Relational Theology is that of praying one for another. Through prayer faith, hope and love are activated in the group and as a result each individual will have new spiritual strengths, both internal and external, that will enable them to better fulfill their ministry.

In the great priestly prayer of Christ that we find in John 17, He prays for us today. We should be open to His example, considering not only the needs of others, but praying that each person may reach the goals of the spiritual life for which our Lord Jesus Christ prayed.

Every Christian is a brother or sister to other brothers and sisters in the faith, also, a helper, a healer, a minister who facilitates the spiritual life of another. As we grow and mature in our life of faith we find many opportunities to help others. This is the way of Christ, and it is an essential part of what it is to be a Christian.

2. Transmit the Realities of the Faith We Hold

We transmit to others the realities of our Christian experience through our relationships. Remember that we have studied this as fundamental to our experience as women. But, how do we relate one to the other? Do we truly feel that a relationship can be the means of transmitting our faith? Needless to say when one life touches another there is a transmission of that experience, a transmission of what is significant for these individuals. We recognize and affirm this truth in the life of the Christian believer through the following two theological concepts:

• **Incarnation.** The incarnation of Christ, when God became human and took on flesh, is a transforming event for humanity. In this event the climatic moment of dialog between God and humanity took place.

"…that is, in Christ, God was reconciling the world to Himself…" (2 Corinthians 5:19a). The incarnation of God in Christ continues today through the work of the Holy Spirit of God in His people. For example, a person can better understand the love of God because another person treats her with love and acceptance. In this way the reality of God is communicated or transmitted through the Christian, or from person to person. It may be through a conversation that God comes to another person through you. He is incarnated in you in order to bring blessing to others. So each believer can say with Paul, "Christ dwells in me" (Galatians 2:20).

The book, *In His Steps*[33], describes a group of persons who were completely changed by the question, "What would Jesus do?" They applied the question to every situation in which they found themselves, and the results were revolutionary! Even though you may not use these same words, the concept here is that of Christ incarnate in you. What would Christ do in the circumstances of your life? This means that wherever you are through your words, your attitudes and your actions, Christ is there incarnate in you. You are the temple of the Holy Spirit, but you also have incarnate in you the presence of Christ and thus you portray what it means to be a Christian to others. You can be a person who transmits your faith not only through your words, but in the way you live your life, in the way you incarnate Christ in your daily life.

- **Community.** In the New Testament the church is not presented as an organization, nor an institution, rather as *koinonia,* an intimate community made up of believers. There is a common life, a life shared among the community. What's more, in the community each person lives in a significant relationship with others. Each one supports and stimulates the life of others in the growth and development of their spiritual life and their service in the community.

Participation in a loving Christian community should provide you, as a believer, a setting in which to experience the following:

- **Responsibility** Assuming and developing a sense of responsibility in your daily life.

- **Affirmation** from those who know you and feel a sense of *koinonia* with you.

- **Support and help founded in prayer** so that you and those to whom you minister may experience healing, renewal, strength and support for ministry.

- **Making decisions** with the counsel of trusted friends.

- **Contentment and joy**, shared and augmented.

- **Reduction of pain** as tensions are diminished.

To be a part of a church is to become aware of the importance of relationships. We do not have to live isolated from others. When you are truly part of a Christian community you find strength for your daily life and for ministry in a group, to that group, and from the group to others. Being part of a Christian community such as the church you learn to transmit the realities of your faith through your life which incarnates Christ ("Christ in you, the hope of glory"), and makes your life and your ministry credible.

3. Being Attentive to the Voice of God.

God does not call us just one time to ministry, but is constantly calling us to new services, to new opportunities to relate with Him and with others who need our help. We must be attentive to His voice and to His desires for our life in ministry. How many times do we limit our ministry because we are not listening to His voice, or that we are open only to those things in which we are interested, covering our ears when the Lord tells us to do something that we do not even want to consider. Being attentive to the voice of God adds a dynamic dimension to our ministry. By listening to Him we can enlarge its scope, learning new ways and achieving new levels of service within the calling He has placed on our lives.

God lets us hear His voice in many ways – in His word, in prayer, through another person, in creation, and in daily activities. God calls us by our name and seeks to have an intimate relationship with us so that we might work together to fulfill His purposes. However, many times instead of deepening our relationship with God, we limit ourselves because of our preoccupations. Many of us should join in this thoughtful prayer, "O Lord, may I not limit you by my own ideas and my feelings which are both limited and limiting. I know that You can do many things through me and with me, things that seem to be totally impossible, such as to bring healing to my spirit. Please help me remain open to the free movement of your Spirit in my life. O Lord, help me to follow You freely and openly so that You can come to me when and how You would. Amen."

The book of Revelation gives us another biblical image about our growing ministry through communion and conversation with God. Christ says, "Listen! I am standing at the door, knocking; if you hear My voice and open the door, I will come in to you and eat with you, and you with Me" (Revelation 3:20.) Here we see the action of God, calling, seeking to be heard. It is only when the person is attentive and hears the voice that she will open the door that permits the relationship of sitting and eating with the Lord and all that that signifies. This is a most impressive picture of the intimate relationship that God seeks to have with each person. In this sitting and eating with the Lord we can understand His vision for our ministry. We can learn to love others as He loves them and find new opportunities of service among them.

We need to carefully analyze the different aspects of our lives to find the reason's for our lack of spiritual development in joyful service to the Lord. Is it that we have not grown in our ministry because we have not been listening to the voice of God? The Bible speaks repeatedly about hearing and listening. The great creedal statement of the Jewish people, the Shema, begins with the words, "Hear, O Israel: the Lord is our God, the Lord alone. You shall love the Lord your God with all your heart, and with all your soul, and with all your might" (Deuteronomy 6:4-5). Time and time again the prophets mention that the reason the nation has so distanced itself from God is because they do not listen to Him. (See Jeremiah 11:10-11 and 25:7 as examples.) And Jesus says, "Let anyone with ears, listen to hear!" (Matthew 11:15) and

> "Why do you call me, 'Lord, Lord' and do not do what I tell
> you? I will show you what someone is like who comes to
> me, hears my words and acts on them. That one is like a man
> building a house who dug deeply and laid the foundation on
> rock; when a flood arose, the river burst against that house but
> could not shake it, because it had been well built. But the one
> who hears and does not act is like a man who built a house on
> the ground without a foundation. When the river burst against it,
> immediately it fell, and great was the ruin of that house" (Luke
> 6:46-49).

Careful listening and hearing God's words includes putting into action His message. We need to listen to Him so that we may grow in relationship with Him as we develop as His faithful servants.

How can I grow in my ministry as a Christian-in-relationship? When I help or facilitate the Christian life in others, when I transmit my faith to others, and when I am attentive to the voice of God to enter into new dimensions of service and development, it is then that my ministry will find new ways of expression and fulfillment as He leads me.

Developing my lifestyle

Not only can I grow in my spiritual life and in the ministry which the Lord has given me in relationship with others and with Him, but also in that which is most basic, my lifestyle. The way I live my life daily is the ultimate test of my relationship with God. If no one sees a difference in my relationship with others, then it is obvious that the relationship with Christ is not central in my life.

As Christians we need to have certain standards for the growth and development of our life in ways that are in accord with the teachings of Christ. We must look for direction as to the lifestyle we should lead, and the Bible is faithful in showing us the way. In continuation we will emphasize some of its important teachings for our growth toward maturity.

- **Walking** A verse that has seems to encapsulate this idea is "If we say that we have fellowship with Him while we are walking in darkness, we lie and do not know what is true; but if we walk in the light as He Himself is in the light, we have fellowship with one another..." (1 John 1:6-7a). The idea of "walking" is used a great deal in the Bible to help us consider and understand the importance of our lifestyle. In two of the best known Psalms this concept has led people through the centuries. "Blessed is the man who does not walk in the counsel of the wicked...but his delight is in the law of the Lord, and on his law he meditates day and night" (Psalm 1:1a, 2). "Even though I walk through the valley of the shadow of death, I will fear no evil, for You are with me; Your rod and Your staff they comfort me" (Psalm 23:4). And again John counsels, "Whoever says, 'I abide in Him,' ought to walk just as He walked" (1 John 2:6). It would be very helpful to make a list of these and other verses which use this concept to study them more carefully and have a broader view of this emphasis so important to the way in which we live our lives.

- **Commitment** As we grow in Christ He is molding us in our attitudes, our habits and our actions toward an integral Christian lifestyle. As committed Christians we are faced with two realities: how we follow the teachings of our Lord and how we adapt to the pressures of society and the environment in which we live. There must be a healthy balance between these two paradigms of our Christian life. Through our relationship with Christ, our obedience to Him, and our sensitivity to the needs of our community, we can have a lifestyle that is authentically Christian but at the same time will undergo change as different situations are faced. This commitment is evidenced dynamically in the Christian women who relates to her community in ways in which Christ would.

- **Service** Our new lifestyle must exemplify the way in which Christ served others. In our world today people are tired of hearing about love and companionship. They want to be able to see and experience love and companionship. They want to see services given in tangible ways: health care, food pantries, feeding centers, compassionate understanding, visits to the lonely and isolated, programs that advocate for justice and care for the oppressed. Our ministry must be responsive to serve these needs in ways we have seen in the examples of Christ. "Let the same mind be in you that was in Christ Jesus, who, though He was in the form of God, did not regard equality with God as something to be exploited, but emptied Himself, taking the form of a slave...." Philippians 2:6-7a). "For the Son of Man came not to be served but to serve, and to give His life a ransom for many" (Mark 10:45). There is never a time in life when the Christian is too old or too young to learn to serve others. The Christian needs to have a sincere desire to serve in the name of Christ, to be trained for that service, and to join with others to carry out that service.

- **Reconciliation** This Christian lifestyle must include reconciliation – with God and with others. Paul tells us that we are "ambassadors for Christ", and have been given the "ministry of reconciliation" (2 Corinthians 5:18-20). Christ teaches us the importance of pardon and of reconciliation with another person. "Therefore, if you are offering your gift at the altar and there remember that your brother has something against you, leave your gift there in front of the altar. First go and be reconciled to your brother;

then come and offer your gift" (Matthew 5:23-24). As a result of these teachings our lifestyle should include reconciliation with God, with ourselves, and with our neighbor. Christians should manifest willingness for reconciliation and even more, they should seek and promote it. Instead of resorting to being aggressive and violent, we must actively promote and search for agreements that are acceptable not only to one side, but also for the other person who is involved in conflict. Being a person who actively seeks reconciliation must be a fundamental and integral part of our Christian lifestyle.

- **Solidarity** Another element that should be found in the Christian lifestyle is that of solidarity. Solidarity means unity with others with whom you have common interests. We need to show solidarity with others, not considering ourselves to be superior or distinct from them, but human beings just as they are. God has created us to live in community and He helps us through the Holy Spirit to do this in ways that stress our solidarity as human beings.

Nevertheless, we must remember that solidarity in our lifestyle as committed Christian women is not just with those who are like us, but God has give us a special ability to identify with the needy and to help them in their specific needs. Christ demonstrated solidarity with the people of His day through His lifestyle. He was known as a friend of sinners, and He gave His life for them. He befriended the marginalized, the rejected, the outcasts, those who were considered unclean. He showed solidarity in healing the sick on the Sabbath. Following His example we can demonstrate solidarity with those who need His pardon and His love. We, too, have these same needs but as Christ's servants we can be the instruments to bring His pardon and love to them. We can share the burden the other person bears, in spite of our own weakness and need, because Christ helps us identify with them, to feel and show solidarity with them. As we show more solidarity with others, as we love more, as we respect others more, as we share in helping supply the needs of others, we ourselves grow more in the expression of our own solidarity. Because He lives in us we receive added strength to act in ways that are pleasing to Him and helpful to others.

- **Hope** Our lives are changed as we become more a part of the lives of others. As a result our lives no longer are embittered, pessimistic, isolating, negative and catastrophic, but rather full of hope. Such a life responds to the teachings of the Bible about the hope that should dwell in us. Consult a Bible Concordance and you will see how many times the word "hope" is found. The Psalms are full of expressions of "hope in God" and the benefits that come to the person who does so. Peter gives thanks to God as he says, "Blessed be the God and Father of our Lord Jesus Christ! By His great mercy He has given us a new birth *into a living hope* through the resurrection of Jesus Christ from the dead, and into an inheritance that is imperishable, undefiled, and unfading, kept in heaven for you...." (1 Peter 1:3-4). We live in a world that is very impersonal and alienating in which hopelessness is the daily experience of many, but if we live a life of hope we reflect the testimony of the light of the gospel and of the love of God. We can become "hope-builders" in the lives of others!

Hope gives a greater meaning to joy, happiness and confidence, bringing new possibilities to life. This is seen in a very special way in the beautiful experience of the two disciples on the road to Emmaus. They are weighed down with grief. Their Lord has died. There is little hope left in their lives (See Luke 24:23.), but suddenly Jesus Himself comes near and walks with them. He helps them clarify their thinking as He teaches them to understand the Scriptures, and finally when they realize who He is, they say, "Were not our hearts burning within us while He was talking to us on the road, while He was opening the scriptures to us?" (Luke24:32). The disciples were filled with joy and full of hope. We, too, can live with hope and expectation in the future knowing that with our Lord every day is full of possibilities, of new experiences that bring us new life and continued growth in Him.

The believer, then, is known by her lifestyle. It should be a life that incarnates the qualities shown and exemplified by our Lord. We must grow and develop with our eyes, our minds and our hearts fixed on Jesus. "Consider Him who endured such hostility against Himself from sinners, so that you may not grow weary or lose heart" (Hebrews 12:3).

Our life is not determined or "set in stone" during the events of our childhood, nor as the result of our sins, but rather as we follow our Lord we have the capacity to make changes, to grow and, to become increasingly the person He has planned us to be. We can look to the future with joy and hopeful expectation knowing that there will be new experiences that will help us in our Christian growth, developing and maturing our lifestyle, enabling us to become the woman God would have us be. In this way life takes on new meaning. In both the failures as well as the successes of our lives we can see how each one can be a step toward a better life. We can say with Paul,

> "If God is for us, who is against us?....Who shall separate us
> from the love of Christ?....For I am convinced that neither death,
> nor life, nor angels, not rulers, nor things present, nor things to
> come, nor powers, nor height, nor depth, nor anything else in
> all creation, will be able to separate us from the love of God in
> Christ Jesus our Lord" (Romans 8:31,38-39).

I'm a Christian woman, created in the image of God. I must grow and develop in all the areas of my life: in the development of my faith, in the fulfillment of my ministry with others, and in my own lifestyle. Relational Theology offers concepts that are basic to a more significant Christian life which will help me pursue these goals for my life. As I increase my understanding and practice of these concepts my service and commitment to God's calling on my life will be deepened and blessed. I can say with Paul, "Thanks be to God for His indescribable gift!" (2 Corinthians 9:15).

Activities for reflexion and learning

1. Review the first section of this chapter, "Growing in My Life as a Believer." Choose one of the four qualities that are mentioned and analyze how you have grown in this area, and why you have been able to do so. Can you apply this information in planning for more growth in one of the other qualities? How?

2. Describe an experience that you have had in a Christian group that has helped you to develop as a Christian. What did you learn from this experience? Why do you think this was a learning experience when others have not been? Have you been able to help another person grow in her Christian life? How?

3. Write down the qualities of a person who is growing in her spiritual life, and those of another person who is not growing. Using these lists, review your own life and decide if there are qualities you have listed that you should add to, or take from your own experience. Will you begin a plan to do it? How?

4. Study Luke 19:2-10 of the experience of Zaccheus with Jesus, noting positive qualities Zaccheus shows in his determination to meet the Lord. Then, note the result of the experience Zaccheus has had with Jesus in the

actions he takes in his community. When we come to know the Lord why is it necessary to make changes that are concordant with His teachings? Are there changes that you need to make that would show more clearly your loyalty to Christ and His teachings?

Questions to answer alone or in a group:

- At this time what is the most important need for your own personal growth as a Christian woman? What will you do to begin to respond to this need and to continue to grow in the Lord?

- What are the relationships that are most important in the Christian life? Why? What steps can you take to strengthen these relationships?

- How can you better transmit your faith in Jesus to others? Describe an experience you have had with someone in which you felt you could transmit your faith in positive and clear ways. What was the difference in this experience from others that you have had when you were unable to do so? What have you learned from these experiences that will help you as you share the "good news" of the Gospel with others?

12. With Eyes on the Goal!

> *"Therefore, since we are surrounded by so great a cloud of witnesses, let us also lay aside every weight and the sin that clings so closely, and let us run with perserverance the race that is set before us, looking to Jesus the pioneer and perfecter of our faith...."*
> *Hebrews 12:1-2a*

One of the essential needs of any person is to have a unifying vision or philosophy for their life, a meaningful goal, something that brings sense and worth to the totality of her life. It is necessary to find and to be able to articulate this vision so that our life can have focus and meaning, but also that this focus can be sustained in moments of difficulty and crisis.

During the Second World War many people were detained by the Japanese, among them missionary Hugo Culpepper, who after the war was a missionary for a brief period in Argentina, and then long-time professor of New Testament at Southern Baptist Theological Seminary in Louisville, Kentucky. Dr. Culpepper says that he had an unforgettable experience on a Tuesday afternoon, March 10, 1942. Among others he and his wife were imprisoned in a Concentration Camp for Civilians in the Philippine Islands. During the previous ten weeks he had lost ten kilos of weight and had suffered a very debilitating dysentery. Along with six other prisoners he had been isolated from the community, outside the walls, receiving only rice water. He was weakening rapidly, spiritually as well as physically. He was almost to the point where it didn't matter if he lived or died.

He began to leaf through his Greek New Testament, looking for words of hope in God, and suddenly he read from 1 John 3:23, "And this is His commandment." A word from God in a moment of crisis! He looked at the words more intently. The passage said two things: "that we should *believe* in the name of His Son Jesus Christ, and *love one another,* just as He has commanded us." He recounts that his heart leaped within his chest. He had something to live for! A new meaning for his life! In the first place the reason for his new-found confidence was the character of God revealed in the nature of Jesus Christ, and secondly, his understanding that what one does with his/ her life should be the result of loving others, and of respecting the inherent value of others who were his fellow human beings.[34]

Each one of us needs to have something to live for, a meaning or vision that is unifying for our personality and sustains us as a person. Without such a vision or purpose, life is very precarious. It can lose its vitality, its direction and its meaning. The Christian woman who knows that she is precious and special in God's eyes must have a unifying vision for her life. She must determine to understand it and develop it. Then she must follow it with dedication.

Inherent in the Christian's understanding of life is a sense of mission. When we come to faith in God through Jesus Christ, our desire is to share the good news with others. In this way the believer participates in the basic activity of God: "For God so loved the world that He gave His only son, so that whoever believes in Him may not perish, but may have eternal life" (John 3:16). The love of God for His creation is the fundamental and eternal basis for all relationships with others.

The good news is that I can find a reason for which to live in this plan of God for His world! I can have a meaningful goal for my life! In continuation we will consider three elements of this vision and purpose for my life: the *context* in which I will develop my life – my world; the *resource* with which I can achieve the goal for my life – talking with God; and a *model* for the fulfillment of my life, the mission given by Christ, being a witness in my world.

The context of ministry: my world

An interesting psychological concepts that is applicable here is that of the "personal field" in which we develop our lives - the psychological context in which "we move and have our being." Every person has his own field and perceives it in distinct ways. This perception is of vital importance in the development of the person. Equally, each of us has a physical and relational context that can be very small and very limited by the way in which we perceive it, or it can be open and growing as a result of our attitude toward it and the relationships that we maintain with others.

The Hebrew concept of salvation is "to be in a wide and spacious place."

This concept helps me interpret my world as a Christian. My field of action is a spacious place that gives me opportunities to share God's salvation and His love and care with others. My physical and relational context is enlarged by my own salvation experience. I am in a broad and spacious place. I have a new world!

Nevertheless, as we have stated previously many times a woman's world is limited by being marginalized, alienated, and not being understood in her desire for fulfillment. Many times it is not easy to be active in her world, but she (along with men who are believers) is called to live in the world in which she finds herself and to apply there the teachings of Christ actively.

The plan of God is that His love reaches out to touch every person in the world, and that through us to all those with whom we have relationships, each member of our nuclear and extended family, every member of our community were we work, study, enjoy sports or recreation, or enter the market place, and through our prayers and missionary efforts to the ends of the earth. This is my world, and in this context I am called into harmonious relationship with others.

We see such harmonious relationships in the Bible. Paul, writing to the Thessalonians, helps them recall "As you know, we dealt with each one of you like a father with his children, urging and encouraging you and pleading that you lead a life worthy of God, who call you into His own kingdom and glory" (1 Thessalonians 2:11). Christ teaches that the most important characteristic of the believer is love one for the other (John 13:34, 35). He teaches His disciples to love their enemies, even those who do them harm (Matthew 5:44, 45).

We are called to live in our world in such a way that others can come to know us as willing to share our lives with them, friendly, interested in them, and willing to be known by them. Our context, since it is relational with both converts and non-converts, requires that we have the ability to establish relationships showing unconditional love to all. Jesus' experience with the woman caught in adultery and His simple and moving words with her, gives us a moving example to follow in our relationships with others as we show them love and concern. "Neither do I condemn you. Go your way, and from now on do not sin again" (John 8:11).

My world, then, is each situation, each interpersonal relationship that I have. It is in this context that I have a special mission. It is here where I can use the spiritual gifts that the Lord has given me.

However, for many people their world can be very small and limited. Frequently this is the reality today. The demands of our agitated, modern life;

the impersonalizing actions of modern technology; the dehumanization of relationships all cause many people to be isolated and lonely, with neither friends nor family, nor significant relationships with others. In the multi-floored apartment buildings in large cities throughout our world thousands live "together", but totally isolated one from another. Many do not know who their neighbor is, and worn out from the tensions of their lives and their fear of entering into a relationship that could make demands on them, they maintain their anonymity, lost in the multitude. They experience what sociologists call "anomie" in which they sense and live disorientation, anxiety, and isolation.

However, the Christian woman finds her world in normal relationships: leaving the realm of anonymity and welcoming life with a smile and a "Good morning!", a "Hello. How are you?" She can show concern as she asks about someone who is not present. She can talk to a child who is playing along the sidewalk. In these ways she can enter into the closed-off lives of others through her friendly approach.

A Christian woman I know of lived in a world of anonymity where no one showed interest in another or "messed in another's business". However, one of her friends had told her that a neighbor was going to have an operation and that the doctor suspected that this man had cancer. She felt that God was telling her that she should visit the man's wife, but she was afraid because she knew how the community frowned on such open "entering into the private life" of another. She thought to herself, "What will the wife say to me? Will she feel that I am doing something that would be unacceptable to her?" But finally she decided that she could not keep from doing what God was leading her to do. The least that she could do was to tell the neighbor that she was very sorry about the illness of her husband and that she was going to pray for them.

Fearfully she knocked on the door and said to the wife, "I am your neighbor. My name is Maria Gonzalez. I heard that your husband is going to have an operation and I wanted you to know that I am very sorry. If there is anything that I can do for you....."

The wife responded, "Please come in," and then with tears running down her cheeks, she said that she was alone, far away from family and friends, and that she was so fearful that she felt totally unable to confront the situation. Yes, she needed the help and friendship offered. Maria stayed with her the next day during the surgery. Her world, and that of her neighbor, had expanded greatly. She had shared her love with another person. She had entered into the ministry that God had for her.

The longer a person is a believer, the fewer non-Christian friends she has. Her relational world becomes smaller and smaller. Even though this can be understood on the one hand, it should not be considered as ideal for the believer who wants to have a mission in the world. It is important to go out "into the world" of others just as God has told us.

What is your world like? Is it small and closed? Does it have barriers and prejudices against those who are different from you? Do you show partiality in the way you relate to others? Or, is your world changing, constantly growing, considering each situation as an opportunity for ministry? The way you perceive your world will enable you to develop a vision and purpose for your life that will help you sustain and unify your world and to be true to your ministry in it.

The resource for ministry: talking with God

The most important factor toward our having a unifying purpose for our lives is a healthy and growing relationship with God. It is impossible to find the mission that God has for us without talking with Him about it. In reality, no one can have a concept of their worth as a person in relationship unless they have talked and dialogued with God in prayer. Without this constant effort our world becomes increasingly smaller, and our sense of ministry and vision gets off course.

God communicates with us through His Word. All through this book we have emphasized that we find reinforcement in who we are as God's special creation through a careful reading and study of His Word. God comes to us through His Word, orienting us and giving us a new vision of who we are and of the world that surrounds us. God's Word is not only a "lamp to my feet and a light to my path" (Psalm 119:105), but, "Indeed the word of God is living and active, sharper than any two-edged sword, piercing until it divides soul from spirit, joints from marrow; it is able to judge the thoughts and intentions of the heart" (Hebrews 4:12).

Thus the Word of God teaches us His plan for our world, what our ministry is within it, and how to prepare ourselves continually to fulfill our role in His plan. We need to read His Word, listen to its message and apply it to our lives.

Possibly one of the reasons why we do not live according to the teachings of the Word of God is that we do not read it as it should be read, but rather in a routine way. We should read it with expectation, knowing that God is going to speak to us through it. We should ask ourselves, "What does this passage teach?" "What does it say to me for my life?" In order to use a more inductive approach it is essential to be willing to listen to the voice of God talking to us through His Word. We must have time to question and look for answers, and a spirit which is willing to adapt the message to our lives.

In Matthew 5, especially in verses 17-48, we find an example of how the Word of God can have new meaning when we approach it looking for its deepest and most profound significance and how to carry out its teaching in our lives. Jesus' teaching here presents an unveiling of the deeper meanings of the law, a teaching that brings new understanding of what it is to follow God's way, not legalistically, but holistically. It should not surprise us that "the crowds were astounded at His teaching, for He taught them as one having authority, and not as their scribes" (Matthew 7:28b-29).

In chapter three we mentioned the importance of the Inductive Method to study the Bible. Review that section and make a more concerted effort to use this method daily so that your understanding of God's Word may be increased and your application of its teaching more continual..

God also communicates with us through prayer. Many times we think that prayer is only what we are saying to God, but we must listen to Him also. He speaks to us when we pray seeking interaction and communication, when we are willing to hear His voice. Today's English Version of the Psalms has the title, "Dialoging with God." The psalmists converse with Him in the most diverse circumstances of life. Psalm 40 expresses in a most dramatic way the result of this interaction with God. Even when one is in the pit of desperation and bogged down in miry clay and he/she cries out to God, He listens and acts: "He drew me up from the desolate pit, and out of the miry bog, and set my feet upon a rock, making my steps secure. He put a new song in my mouth, a song of praise to our God" (Psalm 40:2-3). Read the whole psalm carefully in order to see this interaction and its results.

We need to practice the discipline of listening to God, not only asking that He bless us in special ways, not only to worship and/or express to Him our gratitude, but we need to be quiet before Him, to listen to His voice. Speaking with Him we can find out more about His plan for our lives, and how to carry out His purpose in the world. Our prayer should be, "Lord, open my eyes to see my world, to know and to accept the ministry You have for me in order to fulfill Your purpose for my life." A very helpful thing to do is to discipline yourself to have a special journal where you can write down daily the results of your conversations and interaction with God. In this way you can maintain your commitment by remembering God's words and applying them in your life.

God converses with us through His Holy Spirit that lives in us: He helps us remember Christ's teachings, He guides us in His way, He gives us Christ's words in diverse circumstances, He comforts us in difficult situations, and He promotes our ministry. With so many resources at our disposition, who would not respond affirmatively committing her life to the special plan of God for her?

It is very interesting that the author of Hebrews, writing to Christians who were suffering persecution, cites Psalm 95 two times, "Today, if you hear His voice, do not harden your hearts as in the rebellion" (Hebrews 3:7b-8a and 4:7b). God speaks to His followers; He gives us strength and direction, and is constantly with us, helping us to encounter direction for our lives. Our experience can be like that found in Isaiah 30:21, "And when you turn to the right or when you turn to the left, your ears shall hear a word behind you, saying, 'This is the way; walk in it.'"

God wants to converse and interact with us and in this way to strengthen us for a more meaningful and significant life. Conversing with Him is essential in order to know and develop a unifying purpose for life. Make time for this relationship and this conversation, for God has very special ways in which He desires to direct and bless you.

The model for fulfillment: being a witness in my world

When we come to the point in which we understand the unifying purpose that God has for our lives and for our mission, we need to have practical ways of expressing it in our daily lives. As Christian women we find these ways in the words and examples of our Lord. Christ has given us a commission that indicates how we should fulfill His purpose in our lives. In order to follow His leading we can look to examples of Jesus' ministry that show us the way to carry out our own.

After His death and resurrection and prior to His ascension Jesus gave a geographical framework in which His followers were to carry out their ministry: "But you will receive power when the Holy Spirit has come upon you; and you will be my witnesses in Jerusalem, in all Judea and Samaria, and to the ends of the earth" (Acts 1:8). The field of action for the Christian is found in concentric circles, beginning where one lives, which would be our "Jerusalem" – our home, our community, our city or town; our "Judea," which would be the state, province or department where we live; our "Samaria," areas that are adjacent to our own; and our "world," countries near and far where this ministry needs to be carried out. The world is geographical, it has locality. It is the place in which we are to carry out our ministry, being witnesses for Christ.

But this concept of Christ's mission cannot be limited to geography. The world of Christ was a relational world, just as ours is. Jesus did not come to isolate Himself from the world, but rather He searched for relationships with people that would let them know that the kingdom of God had come near, that all persons could enter into a personal relationship with God and have their lives changed.

Jesus tells us that He is sending us just as He was sent (John 20:21). And so, this is the key we have to interpret the commission that He has given His followers. We find it in the relationships He formed that we see in the pages of the Gospels! Jesus had a mission in Jerusalem, in Judea, in Samaria and in the world. In continuation we will see how He developed His ministry relationally along these lines and find ways of adapting them to our own.

Ministry in Jerusalem

What did ministry in Jerusalem mean to Christ? Jerusalem was the center of power of the Jews. How many times did Christ talk with the leaders of the religious parties, the priests and the people in the area of the temple, striving to have a ministry among them! How many times must He have wept over Jerusalem, the capital of the country, and its religious center (see Matthew 23:37). Luke tells us that, "When the days drew near for Him to be taken up, He set His face to go to Jerusalem" (Luke 9:51). Jesus did not flee from His ministry in Jerusalem, from the sacrifice that He would have to make there.

For Christ to have a ministry in Jerusalem signified confronting the religious leaders of His day and trying to help them have a new vision of what it is to know and follow God. His teachings in the Temple and other parts of the city were an attempt to bring people to a vital experience with God, and not one that would burden them by such a strict use of the Law. But as they listened and even as they saw the marvels that Jesus did, His teaching fell on deaf ears and even hardened their hearts against Him. Jerusalem was the place where many sang joyfully at the entry of Jesus into the city during the final days of His life, but later that week the voices cried again and again a different message, "Crucify Him! Crucify Him!"

For Jesus Jerusalem was not an easy place in which to minister, and, many times, neither is our home, nor our community, nor our church. But God has called us to minister in our Jerusalem, to try to establish relationships with persons with whom it is not easy to do so, with some who will reject us openly. Where is your Jerusalem? What is the ministry to which God is calling you there? Jerusalem, the site of sacrifice, of tears, of rejection, of possible death, - but listen to the voice of Christ, "You shall receive power and be witnesses for Me in Jerusalem."

Ministry in Judea

Judea was the department or the region of which Jerusalem was the capital. It is interesting to look at the map to locate the many villages where Jesus carried out His ministry and see them as a challenge for our ministries. Judea offered Jesus such gratifying experiences as those spent in the home of His friends in Bethany: Mary, Martha and Lazarus. It was a place where He could enjoy a shared ministry, where He could relax and enjoy the experience of mutual companionship, to converse with others who thought as He did, and who shared His vision of ministry. How enjoyable and meaningful were these visits for Jesus, and for His friends. Their importance is underscored when He visited them during the last week in His life, receiving from them encouragement and love as He faced the sacrifice He was going to make of His life.

But in Judea He also had experiences such as the one with Zacchaeus in Jericho. Zacchaeus was considered a traitor to his people since he worked for the Romans as a tax collector. But though he had become rich through the astute and fraudulent use of his position, he was seeking for meaning in his life, and must have hoped that an encounter with Christ might fill that void. It was from his vantage point in the sycamore tree where the relationship of acceptance began as Jesus deliberately took notice of him and said, "Zacchaeus, hurry and come down for I must stay at your house today" (Luke 19:5b). This encounter would lead to his salvation and a changed life. Jesus' personal and caring way of speaking to Zaacheus, instead of the probable taunts and disdain of the crowd (It really was a strange place for a wealthy tax collector to be seen!), His willingness to associate socially with this hated and marginalized man continued in the house and at the table of Zaachaeus. This action on Jesus' part brought Him severe criticism because He was willing to sit down and eat with a sinner such as this hated tax collector! (Luke 19:1-10). To minister in Jericho was a serious and determined commitment for Jesus, but it polarized the religious leaders of His day to oppose Him even more.

For you to go and minister in Judea includes both Bethany and Jericho. You will be able to experience the joy of being with friends who love you and with whom you can share your Christian experience in ways that will benefit you both. At the same time you will be able to relate and share Christ's love with the marginalized of your community, even though as a consequence you may be rejected and opposed for having treated this person as worthy of salvation and ministry. Going to Judea is to fulfill your ministry in areas which are quite diverse: among friends with whom you are comfortable and among the isolated and fringe groups of society where you may be fearful or will suffer because of seeing them as persons whom Christ loves. However, each situation and each area of ministry are essential to the plan of God and the ministry to which you have been called. The voice of Christ comes to us, "You shall receive power and you shall be My witnesses in Judea."

Ministry in Samaria

To go to Samaria means to put aside prejudices and to be willing to relate to people who are different from you, or those considered inferior, or not "pure." The Jews did not go through Samaria, for they considered the Samaritans to be a "mixed race," and thus not "pure" as they were. However, to go from Judea to Galilee, the shorter way was to go through the hated area of Samaria. Usually Jews and Galileans would choose the longer way and cross over to the other side of the Jordan River so they could avoid even walking on Samaritan land, such was their disdain and rejection of these Samaritans.

What was Jesus thinking about when He "had to go through Samaria"? (John 4:4). The Bible says that the Pharisees had heard that Jesus was baptizing more disciples than John (the Baptizer) which would indicate that Jesus had become more popular that John. Jesus, who was not seeking popularity, decided that it was best to get away from Jerusalem and so He decided to return to Galilee. He surprises His disciples when He left Judea and started back to Galilee and chose to go through Samaria. I believe that His decision was not to save time, nor to get away more quickly from His enemies, but rather to fulfill His calling to ministry there, to bring salvation to a whole populace and dignity and a sense of mission to a Samaritan woman.

In this experience Jesus broke various taboos of His day. He spoke publically to a woman, and a Samaritan at that! This was an inconceivable act for a Jewish man (see John 4:27). Not only so, but He also talked theology with her when it was "common knowledge" that women did not have the mental capacity to think or talk of such matters! He asked her for a drink of water which would mean that He would be drinking from the same cup as she, an act totally prohibited by Jewish religious and social laws. He offered her the opportunity to become a believer when His disciples believed that salvation was for the Jews alone.

As a result of this startling ministry not only the woman was saved but she became an evangelist to her whole community when she became a witness saying, "Come and see a man who told me everything I have ever done! He cannot be the Messiah, can He?" (John 4:29). The whole community believed in Jesus and He continued among them for two more days teaching and affirming their faith in His message of good news. Jesus was not afraid to identify with the poor, the marginalized, the rejected and the oppressed, nor even the "half-breeds", the impure Samaritans. He had come to bring salvation to "whoever believed on Him" and here in Samaria He had opened a new door to the Kingdom. His own disciples could not understand His actions for their eyes and hearts were closed to women and to Samaritans, but Jesus continued to show the way of ministry to both groups. To witness in Samaria was a new and challenging experience, but one that has clear teachings for us as His followers today.

To go to Samaria as a witness for Christ Jesus signifies ministry to the marginalized, to the rejected, to those who are considered worthless or "unlike us" by our society, and by us also. Each of us has our own Samaria. Perhaps it is foreigners, immigrants, a despised race, a certain social class, alcoholics, prostitutes, drug addicts, those who have HIV/AIDS, or other marginalized groups. Where is your Samaria? Christ tells us that we must go there to minister, seeking to relate to those we find there, being willing to stay additional time among them, treating them as persons of value and bringing them salvation and change. Jesus says to us, "You shall receive power and you shall be My witnesses in Samaria."

Ministry to the ends of the earth

Christ said, "You shall be My witnesses….to the ends of the earth" (Acts 1:8c). That means all over the world. Perhaps we cannot physically go to a far-away country, or to a little known "people group," but we can have ministry in all parts of the world. I believe that many people have limited their own ministry and have not entered into this broader ministry because they have thought that it is not their responsibility, that they have not been "called" to go to another country. Would this be the plan of God for them, to open their eyes to the world?

The known world in the time of Jesus was not as large as the world is today, and Jesus limited His earthly ministry to the small section that we call the Holy Land. What is the example that He gives us so that we can use it for our own "going to the ends of the earth"? The Bible tells us that Jesus "…went about all the cities and villages, teaching in their synagogues, and proclaiming the good news of the kingdom, and curing every disease and every sickness" (Matthew 9:35).

Jesus' world was every place He found in which to do ministry, to teach, to lead others into discipleship, to bring healing and health. To the people gathered in Cornelius' house Peter, speaking of Jesus, said, "…how God anointed Jesus of Nazareth with the Holy Spirit and with power; how He went about doing good and healing all who were oppressed by the devil, for God was with Him." (Acts 10:38b). The world of Christ was wherever He found a need; each opportunity for ministry was a point on the

Today, our geographic world is closer and our relational world is further apart.

world map of Christ! "He went about doing good" for the ten lepers, for blind Bartimeus, for the 5000 who were hungry after a long day without food, for the epileptic and his parents, for the Gaderean demoniac, for the son of the widow of Nain, for the children who came to Him and whom He loved, for the daughter of Jairus, the ruler of the synagogue, and for many, many others. Christ's world was wherever there was an opportunity for ministry, because His world, as ours, is relational.

There are no limits to our world, or to our relational ministry. In each opportunity for friendship, in each glass of water given to a thirsty person, in each act of reconciliation, in each visit to those who are ill or lonely or imprisoned, in each effort to impart hope and love, each time we listen to a hurting person, in each relationship where we feel that God acts with and through our ministry, there is our world, there we are witnesses "to the ends of the earth."

Today our geographic world has drawn near and our relational world has become more distanced. Images of other people and other locations of the world come into our home through television, and other media. They are as near to us as members of our own family, but the distance between seeing them so near and relating to them and doing something for them is very wide. At the same time even in our family and among our neighbors we have become estranged and the relational distance is wide and profound. Our relational world is "upside down" and at the point of collapse. It needs our dedicated attention and ministry. Without the response of Christians and others of good will everywhere it will continue to deteriorate.

What ministry is God calling you to in this world of yours which is both near and far? Would it be to work creatively for peace and justice, against war and oppression of all kinds, against terrorism? Would it be to feed the malnourished, to offer training for the disadvantaged, to promote understanding among different communities, nations and cultures? Would it be to work actively to eliminate sexual slavery and trafficking wherever it is found? Would it be to give children, especially girls, an opportunity for education? Would it be to be an advocate for those who are abused by their families and others? Would it be to share the Good News with those who do not know of its transforming power? The Christian woman who is aware of her world and of the commission of Christ to minister there will find her niche and follow the example of her Lord. She will join others who are "making a difference " in the world because she is a woman called to ministry, with a vision and purpose for her life.

An additional and very important ministry that the Christian woman can perform is the ministry of prayer. In today's world the number of Christians of all denominations and groups is less than one-third of the world's population. If each Christian would pray daily for two unknown persons in another part of the world, for their needs, for peace in their country, for the health of the family, for their salvation, we would cover the entire world with our prayers! With the images that come to our homes via television and other forms of media we can visualize their faces and our prayers can be more realistic and personal. As women called of God we can enter a world-wide ministry, a concerted effort of prayer for peace and the reign of God in the world!

But we must remember that "my world" includes my family, my neighbor, as well as unknown persons who are in need of my ministry. In "my world" there is a diversity of opportunities, of challenges, of crucial moments, and of crises. It depends on how I perceive them that will determine whether or not they will become a field of ministry for me. In order to perceive and discover my world I need to have the perspective of God. Through daily communication with Him I can reach this understanding as has been already emphasized in this chapter. As I converse and interact with Him, I can hear His words even more powerfully, "You will receive power when the Holy Spirit has come upon you, and you will be my witnesses in Jerusalem, in all Judea and Samaria, and to the ends of the earth" (Acts 1:8).

As Christian women we affirm over and over that we are created in God's image, precious in His sight and essential to His mission for the world. I do not believe that there is a better or more precise model to help us as committed Christian women to fulfill our ministry than this commandment of Jesus. With the relational interpretation of this passage our world draws closer and our ministry becomes more of a daily reality.

Be a committed Christian woman - one who develops her interpersonal relationships as well as her commitment to her Lord and to His mission in the world. In order to achieve this goal, there must be a fundamental commitment of your life to Christ, one that penetrates, orients, and sustains every facet of your life. Without such a unifying purpose and goal it will be easy to lose your way and to spend your life doing many things, but come to realize that they are insignificant, both in your eyes and in those of your Lord.

Thanks be to God that in the mission that He has given us to be persons in relationship we can be strengthened and find direction for our personal ministry through continual conversation and interaction with Hm. Christ is the model for our ministry; He is also the goal. His commission leads us in the way we should go as women in relationship. He has given us a specific mission to carry out in our world. He has gifted us with spiritual gifts and relational qualities that we can use to carry out our mission. He, and our world, await anxiously to see what our response will be.

Activities for reflexion and learning

1. Make a list of ideas and experiences that can help you expand your relational world.

   Doing this will enable you to become aware of the realities and needs of your family, your church, your community and even people in far away countries. As you compile this list if you sense that God is leading you to respond to a specific need, think about how it could be carried out, and what would be the results that you would want to achieve. Note ways in which you could follow God's leadership in this specific activity.

2. What is the unifying and sustaining purpose and goal for your life? How did you come to recognize this to be so? What does it mean to you as a woman in relationship?

3. Write a letter to someone about a ministry that they have done that has blessed you, emphasizing how you recognized this to be a special ministry and the ways in which it has blessed your life.

4. Write a psalm or a dialog with God to express your desire to have a more intimate relationship with Him and that as a result of this relationship you might be able to go forth with more strength and vision to relate in ministry with others.

5. Study the life and ministry of Deborah as a leader of the people of Israel as seen in Judges 4:1-5:21. What were her gifts and abilities? How did God enlarge her world? What were the results?

6. Using Acts 1:8 from a relational perspective as we have done in this chapter, list experiences that you have had in each of these areas. Do you believe that these are a part of the ministry that Christ has given you? If not, why not? Are you able to grow in your vision of the mission that Christ has given you? How? What are some specific ways you can carry out His mission for you?

Questions to answer alone or in a group:

- How can you have more time to converse and interact with God? List at least three specific ways in which your can achieve this goal.

- What are the parameters of your world? Do they need to be enlarged? How can you do so?

- As a result of the message of this book do you feel that you are special as a woman?

  Note at least two ways to confirm your understanding and how you can show God's love in your life and actions.

- What can you do for the members of your family and others with whom you have contact so that they feel that they, too, have a special purpose in their lives? Be specific in ways that you can expand your ministry and help them to find this new concept for their lives.

Personal Postscript

Dear reader,

Thank you for accompanying me in the reading of these chapters, and to think with me about our role as women. I believe that I am a woman created in God's image, special in His eyes, and essential to His purpose for the world. I hope that you join me in this affirmation as well.

I am grateful to God because He has created us in His image and likeness and that as a result our identity is manifested in our relationships with Him, with men, with our family, and our world. In the problems, difficulties and failures we experience, as well as in the joy, achievements and satisfactions of life, the ways in which we relate with others is proof of the fact that we are special. Without a doubt our role in life demands the very best of each of us in each stage, phase and setting that we experience.

How wonderful it is to know that God accompanies us in the development of our lives, giving each of us a more integral and ever-expanding vision of our role as a woman, as well as the strength to reach the fullness of this vision and the goal He has given us. How wonderful it is to know that in all our communities, all over the world, women like you and me rejoice in our special sisterhood, and join in saying with one voice, "I'm a woman! I'm created in God's image. He has a special plan for my life!" May this be your daily experience, dear fiend, ever in more tangible and significant ways.

With affection,

Joyce Cope Wyatt

Bibliography

Gordon W. Allport, *Pattern and Growth in Personality.* Holt, Rinehart and Winston, Inc., 1961, pp. 112-115. Quoted by Wayne E. Oates, *On Becoming Children of God.* The Westminster Press, 1969.

David Augsburger. *¿Diferencias Personales? Enfréntelas con Amor.* Editorial Mundo Hispano, 1984.

Helen Poarch Barnette, *Your Child's Mind: Making the Most of Public Schools.* The Westminster Press, 1984.

Ruth Tiffany Barnhouse, *Identity,* The Westminster Press, 1984.

Sarah Patton Boyle, *The Desert Blooms, A Personal Adventure of Growing Old Creatively.* Abingdon Press, 1983.

Hugo Culpepper, "The rationale for Missions," *Education for Christian Missions: Supporting Christian Missions through Education,* ed. Arthur L. Walker. Broadman Press, 1981.

Erik Erikson, *Childhood and Society. 2nd Ed.,* W. W. Norton, and Company, Inc., 1963.

Eric Fromm. *The Art of Love.* Harper Perennial Modern Classics, 2006.

Robert Frost, "The Death of the Hired Man," Listed in John Bartlett, *Bartlett's Familiar Quotations, 16th Edition.* Little Brown and Company, 1992.

Carol Gilligan, *In a Different Voice, Psychological Theory and Women's Development.* Harvard University Press, 1982.

Anne Marrow Lindbergh, *Gift from the Sea.* Pantheon Books, 1955.

Joseph Luft. *Of Human Interaction.* National Press, 1969.

Jean Baker Miller, Toward a New Psychology of Women. Beacon Press, 1976.

Moltmann, Jürgen. *Man: Christian Anthropology in the Conflicts of the Present.* Fortress Press, 1974.

Henri Nouwen, *The Wounded Healer.* Image Book, a Division of Doubleday & Co., Inc. 1972.

Eugenia Price, *Woman to Woman, 17th Printing.* Zondervan Publishing House, 1968.

Noemi H. Rosenblatt and Joshua Horwitz, *Wrestling with Angels.* Delta Trade Books, 1995.

Letty M. Russell, *Becoming Human.* The Westminster Press, 1982.

Joni Seager. *The Penguin Atlas of Women in the World,* 4th ed. Penguin Books, 2009.

Charles M. Sheldon, *In His Steps.* The John C. Winston.Co., 1937.

Dorotee Söelle, *The Strength of the Weak: Toward a Christian Feminist Identity.* The Westminster Press, 1984.

Paul Tournier, *To Understand Each Other.* John Knox Press, 1968.
Trible, Phyllis. *God and the Rhetoric of Sexuality,* ed. By W. Brueggemann
and J. Donahue. Fortress Press, 1978.

Additional Materials

Article cited in *El Pais,* Cali, Colombia. From class notes.
The News-Sentinel, Knoxville, Tennessee, November 10, 2009, p. A7.
Chart used in classes in Pastoral Psychology, International Baptist Theological
Seminary, Cali, Colombia. Unknown origin.
Class notes, "Ministry to Adults", International Baptist Theological Seminary,
Cali, Colombia.
Data from the United Nations, and used in conferences on the Older Adult,
Knoxville, Tennessee.

Endnotes

1 Jürgen Moltmann, *Man: Christian Anthropology in the Conflicts of the Present.* Fortress Press, 1974, pp. 41-45.

2 Phyllis Trible, *God and the Rhetoric of Sexuality,* ed. By W. Brueggemann and J. Donahue. Fortress Press, 1978, p. 128.

3 Gordon W. Allport, *Pattern and Growth in Personality.* Holt, Rinehart and Winston, Inc., 1961, pp. 112-115. Quoted by Wayne E. Oates, *On Becoming Children of God.* The Westminster Press, 1969, pp. 33-37.

4 Letty M. Russell, *Becoming Human.* The Westminster Press, 1982, pp.19-21.

5 Noemi H. Rosenblatt and Joshua Horwitz, *Wrestling with Angels.* Delta Trade Books, 1995, pp. xx, 14-15.

6 Anne Marrow Lindbergh, *Gift from the Sea.* Pantheon Books, 1955.

7 Joni Seager. *The Penguin Atlas of Women in the World,* 4th ed. Penguin Books, 2009, Selected data.

8 *The News-Sentinel,* Knoxville, Tennessee, November 10, 2009, p. A7.

9 Carol Gilligan, *In a Different Voice, Psychological Theory and Women's Development.* Harvard University Press, 1982.

10 *Ibid,.* p. 129.

11 Jean Baker Miller, *Toward a New Psychology of Women.* Beacon Press, 1976, p. 83.

12 Ruth Tiffany Barnhouse, *Identity ,*The Westminster Press, 1984.

13 Eric Fromm. *The Art of Love.* Harper Perennial Modern classics, 2006, pp. 24-30.

14 Paul Tournier, *To Understand Each Other.* John Knox Press, 1968,

15 David Augsburger. ¿Diferencias Personales? *Enfréntelas con Amor.* Editorial Mundo Hispano, 1984.

16 Tournier, *op. cit.,* pp 62-63.

17 Robert Frost, "The Death of the Hired Man," Listed in John Bartlett, *Bartlett's Familiar Quotations, 16th Edition.* Little Brown and Company, 1992, p. 623:3.

18 Eugenia Price, *Woman to Woman, 17th Printing.* Zondervan Publishing House, 1968, p. 7.

19 Chart used in classes in Pastoral Psychology, International Baptist Theological Seminary, Cali, Colombia. Unknown origin.

20 Class notes, "Ministry to Adults", International Baptist Theological Seminary, Cali, Colombia.

21 Data from the United Nations, and used in conferences on the Older Adult, Knoxville, Tennessee.

[22] Sarah Patton Boyle, *The Desert Blooms, A Personal Adventure of Growing Old Creatively*. Abingdon Press, 1983.

[23] *Ibid.,* pp. 142-144.

[24] Ruth Tiffany Barnhouse, *Identity.* The Westminster Press, 1984, p. 73.

[25] *Ibid.,* pp. 85-88.

[26] Joseph Luft. *Of Human Interaction.* National Press, 1969.

[27] Article cited in *El Pais,* Cali, Colombia. From class notes.

[28] Henri Nouwen, *The Wounded Healer.* Image Book, a Division of Doubleday & Co., Inc. 1972, pp. 87-96.

[29] Helen Poarch Barnette, *Your Child's Mind: Making the Most of Public Schools.* The Westminster Press, 1984, pp. 22-24.

[30] Erik Erikson, *Childhood and Society.2nd Ed.,* W. W. Norton, and Company, Inc., 1963.

[31] *Ibid.,* p. 249.

[32] Dorotee Söelle, *The Strength of the Weak: Toward a Christian Feminist Identity.* The Westminister Press, 1984.

[33] Charles M. Sheldon, *In His Steps.* The John C. Winston.Co., 1937.

[34] Hugo Culpepper, "The Rationale for Missions," *Education for Christian Missions: Supporting Christian Missions through Education,* ed. Arthur L. Walker. Broadman Press, 1981, p. 37.